THE *Glitter* FACTORY

The Making and Unmaking of Sara Picasso

—

A Memoir by **SARA LAVNER**

The Glitter Factory
The Making and Unmaking of Sara Picasso

A Memoir by Sara Lavner

ISBN-13: 978-1499379457

ISBN-10: 1499379455

Book and Cover Design by Alex Schattner

For Bill, who always believed in me.

CONTENTS

PROLOGUE

The Hudson River is calm tonight. The little yellow taxi boat is rushing to Jersey City and the lights on the building across the water are slowly turning from red to purple to white. I can tell what the weather will be by how the currents are moving, rough or still. On the way to fix my tea in the kitchen, I look out the window at the colorful building blocks of the New Jersey waterfront. I watch a large white cruise ship pass by on her way to the Caribbean.

At dusk, sometimes the clouds race in a line against the dark sky and I am unable to sit down. My mind rushes. I must remember to call a patient, to speak with my son's counselor, or to see whether my husband, Bill, has fresh water. The perfume from the late June jasmine flowers seep into the living room. I think I forget something that needs to be done. I'm the only one who can do it.

It feels as if an explosion has erupted in my life and

now I have to find a way to move through the ruins. Much of the dust has cleared, but sometimes I long for the life I had before everything blew up. How did I emerge after the tragedy that befell my family? That will be part of my story.

My husband calls me from the bedroom. I put my book down to go help him. The long plastic straw has fallen out of his travel mug. After I place the straw at his lips, he asks me to close the window and to give him a piece of his favorite chocolate. I smile and lightly kiss his forehead. He has a few beads of sweat above his brow. I see that his wheelchair needs dusting along the edge of the rim. I run my finger over the chrome. Bill doesn't like to interrupt me, but he has no choice except to ask for my help. I am torn between guilt and compassion. I am not a naturally patient person, but I am learning, and his bravery pushes me to find my own. I have come a long way to find acceptance and peace within my life.

My road began in a working-class neighborhood of Brooklyn. When I wanted more than what my parents could offer me, I took the long way across the Brooklyn Bridge into Manhattan to begin exploring. It was a long way that took an unexpected turn when I married a son of Pablo Picasso, a short union that joined me to a world of sophistication and refinement, where I had to navigate the shallows of superficiality, only to discover who I could be on my own. Then I met a man who shared with me the values I thought I had surrendered long ago, a man who reminded me of my roots. And after his accident, I found a strength I never knew I possessed. How I arrived at that strength after my family's tragedy is my story, a story that continues to unfold by the sparkling Hudson but begins in an old New York City glitter factory.

PART I

The Opposite of Glitter

CHAPTER 1

My father worked in a glitter factory for sixty-five years. He spent his days mixing gold leaf paints, weighing the glitter in tubes and supervising the balancing of the brightly colored little aluminum stars that would be placed in glass jars. His arms were strong but his stomach was delicate. He drank a quart of chocolate milk every day at lunchtime to keep regular. He embraced the strict routine of his life.

While he worked full shifts at the factory, my mother sat at home in front of our small TV, imagining a world where she would win all the prizes on the variety shows. Together with my two older brothers, we crammed into a tiny apartment on Bradford Street in a working-class Jewish and Italian neighborhood far out in the Brooklyn hinterlands.

There is a photograph of my mother holding on to my stroller, her hair unwashed and messy in the wind. Her head is dropped towards her arm and in her smile can

you see that a tooth is missing. She is forty-five years old and I am her three-year-old little girl. It's early in the day. She drags me up the four flights of stairs to our apartment as I scream, "Please let me have lunch with the lady across the street!" I keep insisting, trying to break free from her hold. As she struggles to get me inside, tears race down my face. I don't want to be with my mother, I want a lunch date! Then she takes me to the only bedroom in the apartment, plops me on the bed, and locks the door. I continue to shout and cry for an hour. She is tired. She eats her lunch alone.

There is another photo of me at four years old with my brothers, Hy and Victor, standing on either side of me and holding me up, a 1950s sedan in the background. Victor, at five feet eight inches tall, is twenty years older than I am, and my brother Hy, at five feet one inch with blond hair and blue eyes, is fourteen years older. I am looking down the street with excitement in my eyes and you can see how attentive my brothers are with me as they hold me, a curly-haired princess in their arms. There is no pain in my face yet. I don't know what is about to happen when my family moves from this street.

CHAPTER 2

When I turned five, we moved to Van Siclen Avenue, where my bedroom faced the back garden, a space filled with light and roses. One day, I created what I thought was a finger-painting masterpiece with big swirls of color surrounding a small house and a tall orange tree. I woke up the next morning searching the apartment for my painting, running from room to room with a crazed joy filling me. "Victor! Where's my finger painting?" Without looking at me, my brother muttered, "I threw it out." The room became hot and quiet. I couldn't speak.

Now, only in memory could I swim amid the blues and greens of that painting and lose myself in the vibrant pools of color. I could see my desire on that paper, bright and pulsing. I was only five, but I knew I was the only one in the house who could create something that artistic and extraordinary. I wanted someone to appreciate it, to hold it up and say, "Sara, you are an artist! A real Rembrandt!" But instead it was thrown out carelessly, without a thought.

* * *

Within this working-class world, I saw how passionately my mother and father wanted to win things. My father gambled for money by playing card games and my mother tried to win prizes, either on a television show or at the movie theater. And she would drag me into her fantasies with every live television show or matinee we attended. I think she believed that in life she couldn't win, that she was too old or not appealing, but in me, her blond-haired, blue-eyed Shirley Temple, she saw her luck changing.

In 1954, when I was nine years old, my mother took me and our neighbors the Mogilefsky sisters to Princess for a Day, a live variety television show. She had heard that if your daughter were chosen as the princess, she would win a heap of prizes, such as designer clothing and gold charm bracelets. The Mogilefsky sisters both looked like American Girl dolls: perfect white skin, round brown eyes, and a crisp bob of dark hair. That day they wore matching navy blue dresses with white collars and coordinating hats and gloves. I had on a plain plaid dress with black and white oxford shoes and my hair, styled by my mother, was in long ringlets that she pulled tightly in the bath until they spiraled into corkscrews.

When we were seated, the host, Johnny Olsen, combed the audience of expectant young girls and finally selected Elisa Mogilefsky as the princess. Her mother immediately squealed and then shouted, "Take my other daughter also!" The little Mogilefsky dolls marched up to the stage as my mother looked at me with wild eyes. "Follow them!" she blurted, pushing me to my feet, whispering, "Say that you're their other sister!" I quickly obeyed, my face flushed with pink as I neared the stage. There I stood, a small blondhaired, blue-eyed girl with her brown-eyed, dark-haired sisters onstage. Johnny Olsen turned to me: "So, do you have any brothers?" I was paralyzed with fear. My mind began to shuttle between fiction and truth: the Mogilefskys had no brothers, but I had two. In a panic I said, "I ain't got no brothers."

A voice from the audience—my mother's—piercing as a bell, rang out: "Don't say ain't!" I tried to disappear behind the hedge of the Mogilefsky sisters. As our prize, we received a set of hatboxes and little felt skirts with embroidered black poodles. What lessons did I learn that day about my mother's long-buried dreams? I acquiesced to her powerful wish to have me shine, but why was it so important that I be a "princess"? She needed me to stand out from the other children, even if I had to lie on national television, even if I had to pretend to be someone else.

When my mother was fourteen, she became very sick during the influenza epidemic of the 1920s. Her father, a handsome, charismatic businessman and a big flirt (I take after him), nursed my mother back to health. Then he caught influenza from her and died. My mother had to quit school to find a job; four years later, she married my father.

There is another photo: my mother posing in her

rented wedding dress, delicately pretty next to my father, not the most handsome-looking groom. She is only eighteen years old and it looks as if she has lost already. She is getting ready to start a family and run a home. She has no idea that after forty, she will have a newborn to care for, a little girl who she thinks will revive all her dreams.

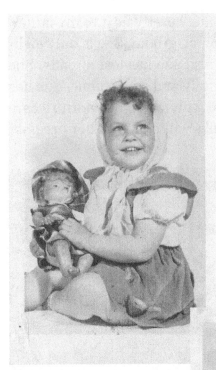

CHAPTER 3

For being a quiet, hardworking man, my father had a very destructive vice. He would often gamble. He had a fantasy of winning big, and although he was exceedingly measured and risk-averse in his routine and diet, he was reckless with his card playing. He would gamble away his entire week's salary; once, he gambled away his entire year's salary. My mother suffered greatly from his addiction. She was constantly worried about money and lived in fear that we might lose the apartment. Gambling was the glitter in my father's private life—the hope that easy riches would find him and his life would sparkle.

Although my father tried to conceal his addiction, his gambling did affect me as a young girl. Often he would bring me pennies and real silver dollars that he had won to put in my coin jar. I felt I had amassed a fortune and now I was a rich and powerful girl. I was very proud of myself for saving up thirteen dollars. One day, my father came home and asked me whether he could borrow some of my money, a sign that he had lost all of his money in a particularly grueling card game. I looked at my full jar of coins glistening on my dresser and couldn't believe he was asking me to give up all that I had saved.

"No!" I said, and he stared at me for a moment.

"You must not be part of my family," he said. "No one in my family would ever do that!" He did not speak to me for an entire week. For many years after, no became a word that would get stuck in my throat, I was at a loss to express dissent to my father or anyone else.

* * *

We always welcomed many cats into our home. When we rented an apartment in a two-family house, I found a black cat that we named Minerva. She and I adored each other. She would wait for me on the corner when I came home from school for lunch. I would play the harmonica for her and sing. She hated the sound and would push the instrument out of my mouth with her paws. All the male cats began hanging out on the front steps when she went into heat. Mrs. Brandwein, the landlady, told my mother that we would have to move if we didn't get rid of the cat. My mother feared we would get evicted. She made me call the ASPCA to have them come and take the cat away to be killed. I went to the phone in the living room, dazed and nauseated, but knowing that I had to do what she so desperately asked me to do. When they came to the door to take Minerva away, something inside of me broke. In that brokenness, I understood that I was the adult and my mother the helpless child. I still cry when I think of that moment and how I could do nothing to protect the cat that I loved so dearly, and how I had no one to protect me. There are moments that are hard to forgive.

I had an intense curiosity to explore new worlds and I was ready to find out how the rest of the world lived outside of my dull home. At ten, when I got on the bus to go to Camp Moodna in the woods of Pennsylvania, all the children were crying. I couldn't understand why they were sad. I was filled with joy, smiling out the window, waving good-bye to Brooklyn, saying good-bye to my mother and father.

CHAPTER 4

"Look, Peter, the sky. What a lovely, lovely day! Aren't the clouds beautiful? You know what I do when it seems as if I couldn't stand being cooped up for one more minute? I think myself out."

I was Anne Frank, looking out my window to the back garden. I was rehearsing a monologue from The Diary of Anne Frank, trying to breathe in the outside, thinking of escape. As I rehearsed, my fantasy of attending the Performing Arts High School grew more possible. Each day I would say her words, over and over, trying to memorize every beat, preparing for the audition that would take me out of Brooklyn.

In the play, Anne is looking for her true friend, and though she is confined to an attic, she is trying to expand her world through her imagination, creating an outside that she hopes one day to enter. She watches seagulls flying outside her window and tells Peter, "Listen to the seagulls, aren't they beautiful?"

A month after my audition, I received an acceptance letter from the Performing Arts High School. I took it in my hand, got on the subway, and rode to the edge of Brooklyn. I got off the train and walked up the long, stone steps to the mouth of the Brooklyn Bridge. I looked out at the expanse of water, the shorelines of Manhattan and Brooklyn, and Staten Island in the distance. I could smell the ocean and immediately I felt bigger.

I stood above the landscape, knowing I could fly over these buildings and this water and land somewhere new. There was a world out there that wasn't sad like my home. I sensed on that day and on that bridge that somewhere people were excited by books, music, and the conversations they had with each other. There might be someone who could see me and let me know that I really existed.

As I stood on the bridge, I remembered the smartest boy in my fifth-grade class, whom I would follow into the library to see what he was reading. One of the books was Gulliver's Travels. When he finished it, I took it off the shelves. Opening the cover, I rushed into these stories. Sitting on the wooden chair by the dark mahogany table in the school library, I felt my heart beating faster as I began the story of Gulliver and the Lilliputians, who were so tiny that it took one hundred of them to tie him up. I would run to that book to read Gulliver's new adventures, about all the new lands he was visiting. I needed to read it, over and over, as if it were food.

CHAPTER 5

In our house on Van Siclen Avenue, my brother Hy would suddenly appear like a ghost from the attic. I would be sitting in the living room on the couch doing homework and he would close the door to his bedroom and practice the violin. I thought he had a secret world in that bedroom, and as the music drifted toward me, I imagined that I could join him and we would play together. I imagined he was my best friend. One day when I began to study the violin he stared at me harshly. "Sara, you are holding the bow completely wrong. You sound squeaky, don't you know how to play that yet?" After that, I stopped practicing and my mother gave the borrowed violin back to the school.

Hy told me that he would look through the keyhole of my parents' door to watch Victor and my father engage in a ritual. Hy said that Victor would remove the belt from my father's pants, hand it to my father, and turn. Hy would flinch as he watched my father whip Victor across his behind and thighs. Hy then stepped away from the keyhole and sat down on the fading brown couch to finish his homework in silence, never telling anyone what he witnessed until many years later.

At first I felt surrounded by my father's love, as he would hold me on his shoulders, posing with me in the photo booth or taking me to vaudeville shows. Whereas my mother had a shy and cautious touch with me, my father was openly affectionate.

When I was five, my father would bathe me on the weekends. He would take the washcloth, put soap on it, hold my back, and then begin rubbing the soapy washcloth on my chest, along my neck, down my legs—and then, wash my vagina. When he would do this, there was a part of me that felt excited and invaded at the same time; it felt wrong, but I didn't know why. It felt good, but I didn't know why. At this point in my life I felt very entwined with my father and it was as if he was putting his mark on me. I think his feelings for me terrified him. Some of those feelings are very natural, but if my father didn't realize that, it can be extremely frightening. The baths continued for a year and then suddenly, the ritual stopped.

Sometimes on the weekends when he wasn't as tired, he would sit in an armchair in the living room and I would crawl onto his lap. I would touch the muscles of his arms and shoulders and declare, "Leave Mommy and marry me!" I was very serious about this proposition and thought it was a good possibility. As I grew older, the physical and emotional intimacy between us seemed to make him uncomfortable. I don't remember his hugging me or ever telling me that he loved me. Eventually, we stopped laughing together.

Then there was Eddie Pearlstein, my first boyfriend and dance partner at the YMHA. We were fourteen and most nights we would go and dance the Lindy together as the Ronettes sang from the record player, filling the room. He would often walk me home, stepping up onto our enclosed porch with me. One night, we lay down next to each other and I could feel his touch on my breasts. Then his lips, and soon we were kissing each other just beneath the windows of the living room. I looked up from Eddie's lips and saw the venetian blind rising, my father's eyes staring down on us. The next thing I knew, he was coming out in a rage to kill Eddie Pearlstein, who ran faster than any marathon runner down and around the block. Once I saw his rage, my father was never the same to me. The mornings became wordless and when he would come home, he wouldn't say good night. I was planning my escape and figuring out how to tell my father that I was going.

* * *

Dressed in my black turtleneck, tights, and mini-skirt, I danced with my friends as the DJ played records during lunchtime, our bodies giving way to a frenzy of swirling motion, never losing the beat. The beats seemed to quicken and intensify, drumming loudly in my chest. I danced with Tamar, a student from the dance department, her hair whipping to the music. Her body seemed to flow like a stream after the winter snow melts. I felt I had found someone who mirrored my desires in some way, a person who felt joy and abandon. She quickly became my best friend.

I would travel to Tamar's house in Queens every chance I got. Off the train, I stepped through the stone arches, the entrance to her magical world of Forest Hills Gardens. Carrying my blue overnight bag on my shoulder, I looked at each home that I passed, each one different and distinguished. I was shedding Brooklyn as my pace quickened.

As I entered her brick home, I could hear her father playing the piano as Tamar danced in pirouettes across the parquet. He would stop playing for a moment, the music seemingly reminding them of something they had shared, and they would laugh together. Then she would improvise a new dance and he would follow her lead.

Tamar's house was filled with paintings and relics from distant lands, and it contained an energy that she and I shared at school. I found her life endlessly interesting, vibrant, and full, her parents always discussing interesting topics with great insight and wit. After dinner, her father played some more on the piano and we danced together. Then the music would stop, her father closing the lid over the keys, and I would leave for the train back to Brooklyn.

CHAPTER 6

In my family I wasn't supposed to concern myself with study—I was an artiste and an actor, of course!—academics were only for my brothers. When I decided to earn my college degree, I was only able to attend night school at Brooklyn College, since my average was not high enough to get me into the day program.

I majored in speech and theater, but my boyfriend, Bob, was heavily entrenched in science and history at the prestigious Haverford College. I spent four years traveling to Pennsylvania almost every weekend with the illusion that I was a Haverford student. While walking around the ivy-covered stone buildings of the campus with two-hundred-year-old trees encasing each hall, I discovered a sweet gentility that I had not experienced before. I longed to be part of that campus and community, but I felt inferior and not up to the standards of the college. Also, Bob implied that I should appreciate that he went out with me instead of the rich Bryn Mawr girls.

It seemed I had been raised to maintain low expectations for my own success. My parents were exhausted by the time I was born and did not know how to nurture a girl who was artistic and sensitive. At my foundation there was a struggle between the grandiose dreams that my mother projected onto me and my deep feelings of inadequacy.

Bob and I decided to go on a European adventure, and when I told my father about my trip, he was very disapproving. "Let me tell you about this woman who works in the factory," he said, settling into his chair. "She comes to work every day, she does her work, and then she goes home and makes her dinner, washes her dishes and goes to sleep, and then comes back to the factory the next day. She never complains." I rolled my eyes. "Do not try to be what you are not."

I did not want to become trapped in my father's cage. I felt intensely curious about the world and I wanted to explore all of it. So with the little money I had, I left for Europe. Even though I felt some guilt, my stronger feeling was to escape my father. There was no glitter in his plan for me.

I met Bob in Germany and felt compelled to visit the Dachau concentration camp. Ever since I'd chosen the monologue from The Diary of Anne Frank, I'd had a desire to understand and be part of the Jewish tribe I was born into. I walked among the sites of the deadly shower rooms and spare bunks and I realized I could have been one of them. I wanted to discover what had happened to my relatives who never left Europe.

One night in the rain, Bob and I hitchhiked with a German man who spoke no English, but lucky or us, Bob could translate. His name was Herbert and he invited us to stay with him on his sailboat on the Bodensei, a lake bordered by Switzerland, Germany, and France. Herbert took us to a casino where there were ladies in long gowns and we ate delicious cheese and bread with red wine. One day he confessed to us that he had been in the color guard of the S.S. troops, but he had run away because he hated the Nazi mentality. I never told him that I was Jewish because I wanted to hear his story, unfiltered and unabridged.

"'I hated the Nazis,'" Bob translated, "'but I was handsome and they wanted to show me off as a representative of the new German people. Near the end of the war, I ran away to hide.'" I had never been so close to someone who had been in the German war machine, and when I thought about how he could have been ordered to kill one of my Ukrainian relatives, I became very quiet. When we parted the next day, Herbert cried softly. Bob translated and told me that Herbert adored me. It seemed Herbert and I felt each other without language. I can still see his chiseled face.

Back at home and in my senior year at Brooklyn College, I had become friendly with a girl named Sandy, who had these deep, oval brown eyes and freckles. Sandy introduced me to a wild city girl named Margaret who lived in Greenwich Village, smoked grass, and would often report on the crazy group sex she was having with her sexy Greek boyfriend. She had an incredibly ferocious edge, as if she could bite a lion if he challenged her. I had never known anyone like her.

Margaret invited us to a New Year's Eve party that took place in a Manhattan loft on December 31, 1967. Sandy arrived at the party before me and met Richard Avedon's three new assistants, one from England, one from Japan, and the last one from France. The assistant from France was Claude Picasso. They were all taken in by Sandy's beauty and instantly wanted to photograph her. I arrived at the party with Bob, after Avedon's assistants had all left.

A week later, when I saw Sandy at school, she came up to me, excitedly saying, "Sara, I met Claude Picasso at the party! I want to introduce you to him. I think he's going to fall in love with you." I looked straight in her eyes and said, "Sandy, why on earth would Claude Picasso fall in love with me?"

"I just know," she said.

In the moment I thought it would be interesting to meet Claude. I figured his life must have been one of parties and adventures, one completely different from my own. I imagined a world of sexy, eccentric artists, so strange and unknown, but seductive nonetheless. I wanted to know about Claude's exciting life, why not! My mind raced through questions: Did he have a French accent? Did he live in Paris in some grand stone château?

When I was in Paris, I stayed in a hostel that charged two dollars a night. I wanted to know whether he would be friendly to me or think poorly of an artistic girl from Brooklyn. Yes, I wanted to meet this boy named Picasso. Somewhere deep down, I knew he would be more than just his name.

A few days later Sandy arranged for us to go to Claude's apartment on the Upper West Side. When she got to my apartment in Brooklyn, she came into my bedroom as I was putting on my makeup and, taking my hand, said, "I need to talk to you." We sat on the bed together. "It's about Bob," she confessed.

I froze and my mind began to gallop.

"At the party last week"—she hesitated—"Bob took me into a different room during the party and asked me to go away with him for a weekend." Immediately my lungs filled with heat and I had a hard time sucking in air. I saw Bob's sad face like a vision in front of me and I wanted to reach out and smash him apart. I was embarrassed but then I thought, why didn't she tell me right away? For some reason she wanted me to know this fact just before I was to meet Claude. Then Sandy hurried me out of my apartment so that we could go to Manhattan and meet Claude. My head was still throbbing with thoughts of Bob and though I couldn't erase the sudden pain, I pretended I was okay.

When we reached Claude's apartment, Sandy knocked brightly on his door. The door opened and instantly

I fell into Claude's large, intense brown eyes. I took in his whole face in one instant, his dramatic cheekbones, his sharp jaw, and his smooth tanned skin. I took a step back to breathe in deeply. Then we followed him into the apartment as his shoulder-length black hair gently swung back and forth. I scanned his slim, muscular build.

As we moved through the apartment, Claude was quiet but seemed fully grounded and his manner intrigued and yet slightly intimidated me. His home was sparse with very little furniture. "I'm sorry," he said, "but we'll have to sit on the floor. My couch, chairs and table haven't arrived." He had a soft French accent with a slight wash of a British lilt from his years studying at Cambridge.

We sat around with some other friends of his and had some wine and cheese. At one point, we began to talk politics. Claude said, "Americans think they are right about everything and want to control all that is happening in the world."

"Please don't bunch us all together," I said, "I don't feel that way." At that moment, I knew Sandy was completely wrong that Claude and I would fall in love. He fascinated me but the glitter of fame began to dim in my eyes and I saw him just as a person, someone very unlike me. After we finished all the French wine and the cheese was down to its rinds, I left his apartment, believing that I would never see him again. I also was preoccupied with confronting Bob and telling him how hurt and angry I was.

* * *

One week later at a party at Margaret's home, I saw Claude again. When our eyes met, we splintered off from the party and ended up standing in the corner, talking all night. The energy around him was quiet but intense, as if there were a sacred well within him that he guarded fiercely.

"So what are you studying in college?" he asked me. I thought his attempts at small talk were immensely sweet.

"I'm a speech and theater major," I said proudly, taking a sip of wine. "I would like to be an actress." This made him smile big and he readjusted in his seat.

"I never went to college. I wasn't a very good student." He looked down and shrugged. "The baccalaureate in France is so difficult, it was hard to pass it, so I took up photography." His honesty seemed fresh and inviting and I felt he could trust me with his small confessions. "Richard Avedon photographed my sister Paloma and me for Vogue magazine and so a few months ago I asked him if I could be his assistant. He agreed and here I am."

"It must be wonderful to do what you love," I said.

"Yes, it is wonderful and challenging. He is a tough boss, but I am learning a great deal."

"Is Richard a well-known photographer?" I asked.

He smiled and hesitated for a moment, looked down, and gently said, "Oh yes, he is a very accomplished photographer."

"It seemed you and the interns really loved Sandy." I held my breath to hear his response.

"Well, we all thought she was very beautiful. But it was James who wanted to date her."

His eyes were like his father's, the ones I had seen in so many photographs, large and full of captured light. His voice had a soft timbre and I was impressed with his honesty and quiet vulnerability. Nothing about him, in the way he dressed or in his casual manner, shouted that he was from such a famous family. We were just Sara and Claude sitting together in a room, getting to know each other. For some unknown reason, which I would slowly uncover, we were comfortable with each other. We seemed to recognize each other and that made all the difference. I wanted to get to know him more but I didn't know whether he felt the same way.

PART II

Sugared Chestnuts

CHAPTER 7

The next day Margaret called me. "Guess who just called and asked for your phone number?"

"I can't believe it!" I sang into the phone.

"He seems very interested."

I had no reason not to believe her. Claude was interested. He wanted to see me again. I felt a rush of excitement at the idea of being with him again, and then some anxiety began to color my joy.

"Well, now I'm very nervous," I told her, and I hung up the phone and replayed my conversation with Claude in my mind. I can't believe I didn't know who Richard Avedon was! I remembered how we spoke so easily of our childhoods and even our dreams. Could he really have been attracted to this girl from Van Siclen Avenue? I couldn't believe it. Perhaps he didn't think of me as a complete philistine. Five minutes later, the phone rang.

"Hello, Sara?" I breathed in deeply. "This is Claude, we spoke the other night at Margaret's party. I wanted to know, would you like to have dinner tonight?"

"Well, I'm home right now and I could make dinner. Would you like to come to my apartment in Brooklyn?"

"Sure," he replied warmly. There was a pause. "Where is Brooklyn?"

I almost burst out laughing but I didn't want to make him uncomfortable. He was showing me that he was up for an adventure, embarking on a new journey to the land of Brooklyn. I was impressed by his courage to explore the unknown. I gave him the train directions and he sounded so eager to make the trip. I began to run around, searching my closet for something sexy to wear. I scoured the cabinets to find something to cook for dinner. He had never been to Brooklyn, he had probably never even heard of Brooklyn, but I was excited he was going to make this adventurous trip to see me, and frightened that he was actually coming to see me. I was sure that he would get lost on the New York subways but he arrived about one hour later at my front door. He was wearing a handsome felt gray coat and held a box of French marrons glacés in his hand.

"Oh, what are these?"

"Sugared chestnuts," he said with a grin. "They are a favorite in France."

I turned the exotic box over in my hands, staring at

the bright inks, the words elegantly scrolled in French. In an instant, I was in a new land.

I had set my small kitchen table with mismatched blue and white plates and paper napkins. I was a bit embarrassed because I assumed, after all the French movies I had seen, that he was used to a more elegant setting. I knew that he lived in a house that had real cloth napkins and large wineglasses, where salad was eaten first and freshly baked baguettes were always on the table. I'd made spaghetti with a store-bought pasta sauce and placed one of my African violet plants on the table. Because I was never allowed in the kitchen of my parents' home, I really didn't know how to cook, so I was a bit unsure how everything would taste. But he politely ate his servings of spaghetti and thanked me. After dinner, I couldn't resist and asked, "May I open the chestnuts? I'm so curious!"

"Yes! Please, please do!" He was delighted. I put one into my mouth and instantly tasted the intense sweetness on my tongue.

"Oh, they are delicious! I love them." He had a huge smile on his face and would not lift his eyes from me. We stared at each another, the sweet sugar still on my lips. Suddenly I got up from the table to get some water and stumbled on the leg of the chair. I tripped a few steps but steadied myself. I took a deep breath. Trying to be casual, I asked, "Had you ever even heard of Brooklyn before tonight?"

"No, but I'm happy to have found it and to be here with you." I glowed a bright shade of pink.

"Thank you. It's amazing you took the subway all the way here, to a place that you didn't know, just to visit me."

"It was no trouble at all, thank you for this dinner." I stood still and smiled.

"Do you want to see my bedroom?" I blurted. "I could show you my books and what I'm studying." He erupted in laughter. Then he took my hand and we went into my room. We walked over to my bookshelf and as I went to get a book, he leaned over and kissed me. Slowly, he began to undress me. I pulled my sweater over my head, revealing my new bra. Then he took off his pants, uncovering his adorable striped boxer shorts. I had never seen boxer shorts before. His upper body was muscular but his legs were short. He took his finger and began to trace my body from my neck down to my hips.

"You are so beautifully proportioned," he whispered sweetly. He studied my body like he was about to draw me. Then we gently made love. I didn't expect this to happen but he was so caring that I immediately trusted him.

We stayed up most of the night talking in bed. He shared his excitement to be working with Richard Avedon and living in New York City. He told me about his grandmother's house in Neuilly and about his sisters and mother, Françoise Gilot. I heard an ache in his voice and noticed his eyes brimmed with a soft sadness when he spoke of his family. I reached down and held his hand.

I never mentioned my family to him. I wouldn't know how to explain them. Even though we were together in Brooklyn, where I grew up, my family felt hundreds of miles away. With Claude, I was entering a new world.

I felt that I could listen to him talk about anything that night, the weather, his photography, sugared chestnuts—anything—just to listen to the music of his voice. Though our stories were so different, and we came to each other from such opposite worlds, I didn't care. We were lying under the same window filled with stars and I thought how far a distance he had traveled to come to me that night, from Manhattan and beyond that, France, to Brooklyn, a world unknown to him, my home.

CHAPTER 8

I had to break up with my boyfriend, Bob. When I told him, he was heartbroken. But he knew that he could not compete with Claude Picasso. He became desperate to get me back. I told him that I knew about his flirtation with my friend Sandy and he denied that it was anything serious. I told him that I was falling in love with Claude. I felt instantly guilty but I knew that I couldn't be swayed by Bob's needs and I had to follow my heart. Through tears, Bob begged me to marry him and move to California, where he planned to become a filmmaker. I refused and he could not accept my decision. He had treated me with superiority from the first moment that we met and I could not forgive him for that. Claude treated me with equality and gentleness and I felt appreciated.

* * *

One of the first times that I went to a restaurant with Claude, I scanned the menu for a long time. He looked at me quizzically for a while. "Sara, what are you doing?"

"Well," I said, putting down the menu, "I don't want to order anything too expensive."

"Please. Order whatever you want."

The most important thing to him was that I got what I wanted. It was the first time in my life that I felt my feelings and desires were important to someone else. My mother's body would seem to cave in when I asked for money to buy an ice cream. She would always go to the cheapest rack in the store and I would be wandering in the other direction to the most expensive dress because it was just more beautiful. I used to raid her large jars of pennies. I was not prepared for Claude's generosity; it didn't feel natural. What I first identified as a common quality between us was a shared neglect from our childhoods, a shared wound. As we got to know each other, he would point out the shapes and colors of the buildings and how the light affected all of our surroundings. There was an enchantment to the world and its objects.

When I first brought Claude home to meet my mother in Brooklyn, I was with some friends from college and she was sitting at the kitchen table in her housedress.

"Mom, this is Claude Picasso." Her eyes went blank.

"Picassio?"

"No, Mom, Picasso."

"Nice to meet you," she said, sticking out her plump hand.

A few months later, I brought her a book of Claude's father's sculptures.

"I am not showing this to your father," she whispered coarsely.

"But, why not?" I asked.

"He has to do so many nude women?"

I laughed. I had an instinct about art and beauty from an early age; I believe I was born with it but it was not there for my parents. At that moment we were not only speaking different languages but we were in different centuries. Claude was amused by all of this; maybe he had never met someone who didn't know who his father was and maybe it was a relief. My mother and father looked at Claude as a young man and responded to his kindness and sincerity with them. My father did not care at all about Claude's fame and though my mother slowly began to understand, she brought him her stuffed cabbage in insulated bags. They didn't care that he wasn't Jewish or from their world; they took him in as family.

I didn't feel frightened by the people I was meeting through Claude, even though some of them were quite famous. We spent many weekends in the Hamptons when it was filled with artists de Kooning, Steinberg, Gottlieb, and many more. We used to stay at the home of Tony Rosenthal, whose cube can be turned on Astor Place. I helped Tony paint it several times. We were invited to all the parties with the artists and the collectors. Saul Steinberg lived down the road from the Rosenthals in the Springs. He had a wonderful Romanian accent and was the most playful of all the artists. When I visited, he would make up stories for me. Claude and I adopted a cat from the market, an orange tabby, and I named him Solito, after Saul.

Tony Rosenthal and his wife Helena took on the role of godparents to Claude and me; we were both looking for parental figures who would give us lots of attention. They gave us a little house on their property where we stayed on weekends. At Laos Point, a beautiful inlet in the Hamptons, we would spend hours lounging on the beach with the artists and writers. Saul Bellow used to rent a house nearby on the road to the beach.

"When I was a young man," Saul said to me one afternoon, sitting in the sand, "I had a strong desire to meet Trotsky." He looked away as though caught in a distant place, and his voice slowed and deepened as he continued. "After the revolution, Trotsky had to escape to Mexico because Lenin didn't want him in Russia." He looked down, enveloped in memories. "You see," he explained, "Trotsky was in danger of being harmed. So, I decided to go to Mexico to see him." Then he was quiet. I sensed a heaviness come over him. "When I arrived,

I found out that Trotsky had just been murdered." As I listened to him, I felt I was entering a world where people like him lived out their fantasies, where imagination fueled a passionate way of living. Maybe I could live here, in the sudden joy of creating a new life for myself. Maybe I could create a new history.

I kept absorbing the stories, attitudes, and language of these artists. But I was still invisible to most of them. At a party, a woman in a champagne Chanel suit with a long string of pearls walked over to me. "It's so nice to see you again, my dear," she said with a wooden smile. "Hello, it's nice to see you," I said, not sure where to look. "Oh my! Your English has really improved." I muscled a smile, offered a thank-you, and left the room. At that moment, I was beginning to understand what Claude had meant when he said that having the name Picasso was like opening a Pandora's box. "I don't want to marry you," he once said, "and have you live with the burden of the Picasso name. You don't know what it's like. It's a burden that I was born into. I have no choice." He paused and thought deeply. Then he looked at me. "But you have a choice."

The woman in the champagne Chanel suit could not see me as a real person. In her imagination I was some French girl from a wealthy family, now joined to the Picasso family. The Picasso name had an aura that blinded people, making them behave artificially, sometimes cruelly to me. I could understand Claude's pain and confusion from a life of encountering these types of characters. Above all, he wanted to protect me from getting burned in the scorch of the name.

One night we were invited to the home of Paul Rosenberg, the son of Picasso's first art dealer in Paris. We ate at an old maple table set with Limoges plates and Christofle silver. Their bird, a macaw, imitated the sound of venetian blinds opening and closing. After dinner, Paul showed us the invitation to Picasso's first art exhibition, a real piece of history, in his library of rare books. I was looking at books transcribed by monks from medieval times wrapped in old chains and locked to a pedestal. It was the oldest piece of antiquity I had ever seen outside of a museum. As we toured his library, Paul looked at us with a great smile. "Let me tell you about my father and Picasso." Claude and I leaned in, sipping our wine from sparkling crystal.

"My father went to the South of France to visit Picasso. As he stood outside of his estate, he kept ringing the bell. After several minutes, the doors finally opened and my father walked through. When he got inside, he asked Picasso, 'Why didn't you allow me in, dear friend?' 'Oh,' Picasso responded, 'I thought you were the tax collector.' "

After that night, I remembered some of the stories that Claude had told me about living with his father. Once when Claude was about fourteen, his father gave him some money to buy him some cigarettes. When Claude returned to the house, he brought many gifts and different food items besides the cigarettes. His father was astonished, "How did you get so many things for so little money?"

"Papa," Claude said, "that is how much money you gave me, it could easily buy all these things."

"I hate you because you are so young."

These stories were a window into knowing Pablo Picasso and, by extension, Claude. I was falling in love with Claude Picasso and I could feel a deep connection to his honesty and his sadness, too. We both felt so distant from our families; we were alone in the world, trying to create ourselves anew. We decided to create a new family together.

CHAPTER 9

It was summer in the Hamptons. While we were staying with the Rosenthals, I would ride my bike over to de Kooning's house off a remote road. My bike slid into a slim opening within a wall of tall hedges and as I gazed into the house through the large picture window, I would watch de Kooning working in his studio. At twenty-three, I found him incredibly attractive, my first taste of the older man. He was studying his latest painting, sitting in a chair that looked like a throne. I watched his stillness and focus. For a moment I thought of going in, and then decided I shouldn't disturb him, but I couldn't stop watching him. It was like entering someone else's dream.

De Kooning told me that he built his house to look like a ship. In his youth he worked on ships and always thought he would design a house that looked as if it could go out to sea. He opened his closet door to show off a fleet of exquisitely padded hangers. With their acquisition, something seemingly insignificant but so luxurious, he had made it as an artist.

* * *

"You are going to meet my mother," Claude said when we arrived back home in Manhattan. "She's flying here in a month." I choked on the water I was drinking. Who was this mysterious woman, Françoise Gilot, with such a past, and what will she think of me, his American girlfriend?

Soon we were driving to the airport to pick her up. She appeared like a vision, a stunning darkened silhouette with piercing hazel eyes, one eyebrow higher than the other, and dressed head to toe in black leather and adorned with gold jewelry.

She looked at me with a faint purse of her lips. She mumbled a hello. I felt like a pauper in my paisley skirt and cotton blouse. Her coolness came off as fierce judgment so I tried my best to say very little. I wondered what Claude thought of having a mother who looked poised as a Parisian supermodel. I didn't know mothers could look like that.

We brought Françoise to her friend's apartment on the Upper East Side. When we brought in her suitcases, her host actually walked with his nose slightly tipped up in the air. And they never looked at me during the entire time we were there. We went to dinner with Françoise and she was polite but she also never spoke to me directly. Maybe they all thought that if they ignored me, I might just disappear.

When we parted at the end of the night, I exhaled a

great big sigh. Claude never seemed to be disturbed by their treatment of me and I didn't have a strong enough voice at the time to confront him about his acceptance of their dismissive behavior. I think this withdrawal was especially rooted in how my brother Hy would make me feel insignificant, dismissed as silly or dumb.

* * *

During our first year together, Claude's sister Paloma came to visit. I had no steady work and would sometimes do an acting job, so I had a lot of free time. At this time, an heiress to the Lilly pharmaceutical company invited Paloma and me to stay at her private island on Lake Michigan. I had no clue as to how rich this woman was, my naïveté kept me innocent of many such situations. Her much older husband, Vasek Simek, was a Hungarian theater director who decided to make a film with her and it became clear to me that he was using his wife's money and really didn't care about her. He was a modern-day Svengali; he had a mystical dominion over her and her money. He was able to convince her to bankroll all his films. He had her doing scenes over and over again until she was completely exhausted. Finally, during one of the scenes in the movie she accidentally broke a glass and fell on it. She was nervous and wanted to please him. There was a sense of danger in the air; I felt that something out of control could happen at any moment. Paloma just let everything slide off her; she had some kind of protective shield that was foreign to me. Paloma would say very little, as though she didn't want to be pinned down and

known. She had a smile like the Mona Lisa; I was never sure what she was really thinking or feeling. Flatly, she declared, "My parents never married. I am a love child."

Claude had really missed me while I was away. Before I left for the island with Paloma, I was feeling distant from him. It was a summer morning, and as I was unpacking my suitcase, Claude came and stood in front of me, his vibrant brown eyes sparkling with intensity. "I want to marry you, Sara." I stopped folding clothes and sat on the bed. "But when I left," I said, "you said you would never marry me because you don't want to burden me with your name. What happened?"

"I missed you so much while you were in Michigan. I realized I wanted to be with you always. I want you to be my wife." I picked up a few blouses and began refolding them. My hands were busy, my mind racing.

"But I don't want to make a big deal of it," he said quickly. "I don't want anyone to know, so let's do it at city hall."

"Well, we can do whatever makes you comfortable." He held me especially tight and then gave me his most charming smile. I didn't care about wedding presents or gowns or invitations, I just wanted to be a permanent part of his life. I wanted to join the world that he had introduced me to and in that moment, I forgot about the Pandora's box and all its dangers. I felt safe with Claude, who would soon be my husband.

* * *

During our engagement, I used to sneak into the bathroom and secretly read Claude's mother's book, Life with Picasso. I wanted to understand where he came from, what life was like for his family, and what characters filled his home. Maybe we shared the most important thing, the central feeling that transcended status or fame or riches, what is at our core: how our parents treated us. And from that treatment, Claude and I shared a similar wound, a feeling of being ignored and unimportant. We were both searching for what was never seen or valued by our families and we attempted to find it in each other.

One day Claude caught me. "Oh, you're going into the bathroom to read my mother's book." The more I read about how he was treated, the more I understood him.

* * *

That summer we spent a great deal of time in the Springs of East Hampton. There was a natural inter-mingling among the rich collectors, the artists, and the townspeople who had always lived there. The summers were sprinkled with bicycle rides, beautiful beaches, and a special light that bathed everything in its muted glow. I loved being there, I felt at peace, even my hair was relaxed and curly. "Stop straightening your hair," Claude would say, "I like it curly and wild. It's natural." He appreciated my natural beauty.

Claude loved photographing me. We would be sitting around the house, sipping tea by the window, as the day was running out. Suddenly he would get this sparkle in his eye and shout, "I have an idea, I want to take your photo right now!"

He'd then race around the bedroom, grabbing my short skirt, my silky blouse, the silver medallion his father etched for him. In the summer heat, I was anxious to be outside. My hair would explode into a mass of frizz. But I wanted to help him in any way I could to allow him to find his own artistic voice, to fuel his desire. There was a moment when I felt like a prop for him, remembering my mother sticking me in little dresses and parading me around theaters or television studios. But I felt more like his partner, and for the first time I was an inspiration for someone.

His eyes glowed as he gathered his equipment. "We'll

go to the promenade, along the water, I want to photograph you there." When we got to the river, my hair was flicking in the breezes off the water. He instructed me to dance in place, as my curls whipped around like the current beneath us. I went on my toes and became a ballerina for him, bowing as if an audience were watching my every move. His camera clicked along. I thought he had taken a thousand shots and then he suddenly stopped. "Good," he said, "very good." And he put his camera away.

This would become our ritual. We would venture outside, right after my shower, when my hair would be his favorite, wild. He took a mirror, shined it into my eyes, and snapped away. There is a photograph he took that looks like a Renaissance painting. I can see his energy and passion when I look at that photograph. I see his love for me, his desire for my body. His talent was alive and inspiration seemed boundless. This was when he was happiest.

As the summer drifted, I noticed that some days, Claude would be very funny, imitating our cats, and laughing with me on our bed. But other times, he appeared intensely sad and withdrawn. One night, we went to a party at the home of George Plimpton, who decorated his loft with a bevy of live black swans. I walked in, my hair curly and free, my body draped in a long cotton, tie-dye dress, and immediately I eyed a very attractive couple entering the sunken living room. It was Warren Beatty and Julie Christie.

Later in the evening, Julie and I ended up sitting upstairs in George's small study on an embroidered couch, drinking wine. "You looked so beautiful," she admitted, completely engaged. "I was drawn to you." I blushed. "I love your curls!"

We talked for a long time, exchanging stories about our lovers. "I would sacrifice almost anything for Warren," she confessed. It sounded romantic, but I sensed weariness in her voice, as if she felt a slave to his love. I wondered whether I, too, would go to any length for Claude. How was I enslaved?

When we left the study, Warren was flirting with a few women in the living room. Julie went to hide out in a different room. I was at the punch bowl and I felt a hand on my back. "Hi, I'm Warren, what's your name?"

"I'm Sara," I said. He smiled while he sipped his punch, staring into my eyes over the rim of his glass. I followed him over to the couch, where five or six other women all welcomed him back. He talked about his latest project, a film he wanted to make about John Reed, an American journalist and Communist who went to live in Russia. He spoke with such unbridled enthusiasm, his beauty filling the room. I said, "Oh, wasn't John Reed that radical reporter? He was a brilliant man." Warren smiled and turned to me. "She's smart." He had seized all of my attention as well as that of the other women in the room. We could not resist him.

As the party ended, Julie and Warren and a few others went to Elaine's restaurant and invited Claude and me to join them. Claude was enraged. He refused to go. I stood in the street, leaning on the gate near the apartment house, imprisoned by his refusal. I could feel him tightly pulling my reins and I was beginning to champ at the bit. Then it hit me. Claude was the one who decided when we left a party, he decided how we would get married, he decided what we would buy for our home, and he decided who mattered and who didn't.

CHAPTER 10

"Let's go to city hall," Claude declared. It was January 1969. I called my parents. "If you're not busy, come to city hall because I'm getting married tomorrow." My father's breathing quickened. "What are you doing? You never told us! You haven't invited your brothers?"

"No, I haven't invited them." No response on the other end. "If you can make it, meet us at city hall at noon." He hesitated and then said, "We'll be there."

When I hung up the phone, I felt uncomfortable. I heard the hurt breaking my father's voice. In that moment, I decided to wear a white dress that my mother had once knitted for me. But I didn't feel myself in that dress. I wanted my parents there and I didn't want them there. I cared about them, and I didn't care about them.

Claude was nervous about anyone knowing about the ceremony. He demanded that it would be quick and quiet. I felt that I had to follow his lead. I could hear a murmur of something being wrong, but I tried to ignore the sound.

We sat on plain wood benches surrounded by every ethnic group in New York City. Then we went into a large empty room and a stranger married us. Afterward we had lunch at a restaurant on top of the 666 building on Fifth Avenue. My father called my brothers; with his voice tight and restrained, he told them that I had just gotten married. Then he made me get on the phone to speak with them. They didn't know what to say.

The night of my wedding, Claude, his friend Marie, and I went to see the film Romeo and Juliet. Marie was with us on our wedding night—what is wrong with this picture? As we went home on the subway, my wedding day felt anticlimactic and there seemed to be something missing.

When Claude called his mother to tell her, she was extremely upset. She had told him that he couldn't marry me because we were not of the same class. Of course I knew how Françoise felt about me: Claude had reported her disapproval a month before we got married. Then she wrote him a letter after we were married. She stated that she didn't want to see him anymore or have any-thing to do with us, but if we met her at a party she would of course say hello. I couldn't believe that a mother who knew all that her son had been through, with his father's refusal to see him since he was seventeen, could write such a letter. No matter what I did, my parents never rejected me in this way. I couldn't believe she would hurt Claude so intensely. Claude appeared hurt but did not show very much feeling about it, so it seemed he was used to this kind of treatment.

I was furious with Françoise and very protective of Claude. I decided, with his permission, to write a response to her. I told her my exact feelings of disappointment and sadness about how she was hurting her son and I mailed it off. A few months later, when we visited Paris on our honeymoon, as I entered her bedroom on the top floor, I spotted my letter, tossed among papers and sketches on her desk. There it sat, open like a wound. I wanted to know why she had kept it, but never felt that I could approach her about it. She always maintained a fence around her and I didn't know how to unlatch the gate.

"You have to understand something about my mother," he said to me one morning after the letter arrived. "She's always been opening and closing doors with me." His eyes were dry, his voice clear. "When I was young, my mother was painting in her studio, the door always locked. I kept asking to come in but she kept refusing. Finally, I said, 'You are a better painter than Daddy! Please let me come in!' In that moment, she opened the door."

PART III

Outside the Gate

CHAPTER 11

"I would like you to meet my father," Claude said to me one day after the wedding. "It's been five years since we last saw each other."

Finally I would get to meet the great Pablo Picasso, a man I knew intimately through Claude's stories. Would he be larger than life? Would he show me his studio? Would he be nice to me? It was all unimaginable.

We planned to honeymoon all over France, ending our trip in Mougins, where Claude would have a chance at last to reconcile with his father. When we arrived in Paris, we stayed at a romantic little hotel near Notre Dame where we scaled a narrow stairwell that spiraled up to a quiet attic room. Once we settled in, Claude was busy with some papers. "I have some banking business to do." He smiled and kissed me. "I'll be back in a few hours." I was able to relax in this cozy retreat and read Agatha Christie detective novels by lamplight.

The next day, Claude called his mother to set up a

meeting at the home of his grandmother in Neuilly, a fancy neighborhood near the Bois de Boulogne. "I will see my mother alone," he told me, "and then after about two hours I want you to take a taxi and come to join us." I fell silent and slowly exhaled.

"Don't worry," he said, "she will be fine with you."

Claude's grandmother's house, built around the Art Nouveau period, rose like an urban castle in front of me, with massive stone walls and an ornately designed iron gate around a large garden teeming with bougainvillea. As I rang the bell at the gate, I saw an older woman walking down the street holding a small black leather handbag and wearing an old-fashioned chapeau draped with netting on the side. Very elegant, I thought. Our eyes briefly met, then suddenly she turned around and walked away. Then I heard the buzz of the gate and I walked into the house. Inside, it was quiet and dark. I peeked down the empty hallway and saw no one. I knew Claude's mother lived in the attic, so I took a chance. I climbed the winding stairs to the attic and walked through a door to a spare room with a simple bed, a couch, and a writing desk. Picasso's famous painting of Françoise as a flower hung over her bed. I had never been in such close proximity to such an expensive piece of art outside of a museum. My eyes took in every inch of Françoise's quiet retreat. I noticed the letter I had sent her was sitting on her desk, opened.

Françoise and Claude were in the middle of talking about important matters and seemed to ignore my presence. This attic room felt so far away from the rest of the house, so why did she live in the attic? Like Claude, was she also an outsider to her own family?

"Sara, my mother and I still have some things to discuss," he said, "so why don't you go down to the garden and I'll meet you there." He never reintroduced me to her and I left the room. As I began to walk down the staircase, I saw the same older woman with the fancy chapeau I had seen outside the gate. She was climbing up the stairs and our eyes met again. "Je m'appelle Sara," I said, gentle-voiced. Without a word she brusquely walked past me to her room at the end of the hallway. That was my first meeting with Claude's grandmother.

I continued down the stairs and wandered into the garden, feeling the chill. I wondered what else was in store from this group of cold women. By marrying Claude, I had officially joined this family, and by entering their home, I realized I needed to brace myself for the unknown. This bizarre family life felt somewhat normal because of my estrangement from my brothers and parents. But I was upset. I quickly jumped from one flower bush to the next, not quite knowing where to stop and breathe, trying to calm myself.

After fifteen minutes, Claude joined me in the garden. "Come back inside."

"But I feel hurt by your family's reaction to me." I had told him about my encounter with his grandmother.

"I'm sorry," he said softly, "they are angry at me for getting married without their permission." He smiled like a coach encouraging his team. "We have to go back upstairs to see them for just a little while, or they will be very upset with me, and then we can go."

We climbed back up to the attic and found the whole family gathered in Françoise's room to meet me. I met Claude's ten-year-old half sister, Aurelia, who was from Françoise's marriage to Luc Simone, the man she married after she left Picasso. Then Claude introduced me to his grandmother, who still wouldn't look at me.

"Where is my dog, Harry?" Claude asked his grandmother. "I want Sara to meet him."

"He died," his grandmother snapped.

Claude stepped back, as if someone had knocked him square in his chest. There was a long silence as he stared at the floor. He muttered something in French, something I didn't understand. After a few more uncomfortable moments we left the house. In the taxi back to the hotel, Claude kept shaking his head.

"Why didn't they tell me?"

"I can't understand why your grandmother must be so cruel to you, I'm sorry they treated you that way. I feel it is my fault that they are angry with you." I reached for his hand.

"No, no," he said, "it's not your fault, they can be very

mean."

I felt so badly for him and found the introduction to his family so startling. Who were these people? They clearly wanted nothing to do with me. Maybe we don't need them! At the same time, I wanted their acceptance but didn't have a clue how I would get it.

That night we had dinner with Luc Simone at a small Moroccan restaurant on a narrow street with worn cobblestones. Each facade had a dark wooden door—it looked like an illustration from an old Parisian picture book. Luc was tall and dashingly handsome, like a model from a vintage cigarette ad, and spoke haltingly in English. He was the most welcoming of anyone so far and was delighted to meet me. Luc's family had been stained-glass window makers for centuries from a town near Chartres in France. Luc was my fantasy of what a French artist would be like: casually but fashionably dressed, with a twinkle in his eye. I was delighted to be in his presence. Claude was also happy to be so embraced by Luc.

The next day, I met Claude's older brother, Paulo, Picasso's only legitimate child. Paulo's mother was Olga, a Russian ballet dancer, who married Picasso when he was a young man. We had lunch with Paulo's second wife and young son. The famous painting of Paulo as a child with blond hair, wearing a white bonnet and a blue outfit, looked down on us while we ate. It felt like a dream to see it at the home of the person who was in the painting, my real-life brother-in-law. I kept turning to the painting to make sure it was still there. Yes, I reminded myself, I was still having lunch with it. Paulo was much taller than Claude and didn't look like him at all. He seemed gentle and spoke only French. Paulo told us that he would call his father in the South of France to tell him about our marriage. He also said he would arrange for us to meet with him. Claude feared that his own phone call would not be taken but knew Paulo would get through to their father. They spoke quickly in French about what Paulo would say and he told Claude that he was sure that his father would be happy to see him and his new bride. Claude appeared hopeful that we would get to see his father, whom he had not seen in five years. Even though Paulo was hospitable and accepting, there was a certain formality to our luncheon, emanating from his bourgeois wife. She looked me over with cool eyes in her beige Chanel suit. I felt that she didn't trust me. On the other hand, Paulo was warm and caring. Paulo was very emotional at the thought of us meeting his father. He wanted it to work out for Claude and this made Claude more hopeful.

As we descended in the old caged elevator, Claude said, "You know Paulo was employed by our father as his chauffer."

"What! He was your father's servant?" I gasped.

Claude said stoically, "Yes, he worked for him for many years."

"Why would Paulo do such a thing?" I asked.

"He wasn't very good at school but he loved working on cars and so he worked for our father." As we left the building, Claude leaned over. "I think he will actually call."

"I hope so," I said, "I really hope so."

"We'll go to the South of France, to see him," he said, and he squeezed my hand.

* * *

A few days later, we traveled to Luc's five-hundred-year-old country home, located in a little village outside of Paris. Claude and I walked outside around the house. "Oh, la vache!" I squealed when a cow came up to me, having no idea I shouted an old French expression. Everyone laughed at the American girl. Coming from Brooklyn, I'd only encountered a cow in the butcher shop. It was a relief to be laughing, surrounded by such warmth after a week in Paris with Claude's chilly immediate family. The countryside looked composed, like an old French pastoral painting, with hills peppered with grazing animals and meadows overtaken by butterflies. "You know," I whispered to Claude, "I've always wanted to be a butterfly."

"Why? They only live for one day."

"That is exactly the reason." I beamed. "They emerge from their cocoons and live fully just for that day."

Those butterflies, skimming the low bushes and the

mustard-yellow wildflowers, represented something more to me. They were freedom. Those little beings were kites to the air, floating and diving in the breezes, searching for something sweet to drink. They had purpose and they took action. I was longing to do just that in my own life.

Some of Luc's friends, artists who owned country homes nearby, came over for a fondue dinner. There was plenty of Bordeaux wine, and we all sat very close to the giant fire and laughed and dined all night. At night we had to sprint down the hallways to escape the cold, and warm ourselves by the large fireplace in our bedroom. We dove under the covers into each other's arms. Claude embraced me, his hands sliding along my back.

"I'm so happy Luc was so warm to you," he said, his voice finally sounding calm and settled. "I really love him." I kissed Claude along his neck as the fire blazed within our room, sending jumping shadows to the ceiling.

* * *

The next day, Luc planted a young rosebush in his garden to commemorate our marriage. I loved how old and new it all felt to me: an old French village with the promise of new life. And a new family I was growing to love. Luc smiled at me as he tamped down the soil with his shovel. "Now you can have roots in our family."

CHAPTER 12

Back in Paris, Claude's friends were very curious to catch a glimpse of Claude's American wife. We were invited to the home of the family's doctor, a house that made me feel I had gone back in time. We ate at an antique round walnut table with beautiful china and crystal wineglasses. A maid came and served us five courses. The doctor's wife was quite old and hunched over but spoke to us gently. She was a handwriting expert. "Write down something," she instructed us, "I'll give you an analysis in a few days."

Later that week, after a visit to the doctor's wife, Claude met me on the steps of Le Madeline. He came barreling up the steps, flashing a piece of paper in his hand while his eyes darted angrily. "She says you are very creative!" he growled.

"Don't be silly," I said, "yours is just as interesting, but in a different way."

"No, look!" he said, his hand rattling the paper.

"Yours is better than mine."

I took his hand and we sat down on the steps. We were quiet as I read her analysis: "Sara is as light as a butterfly and extremely expressive." When I read that his handwriting seemed to be average, I was worried about his feelings. Even though I was delighted about my handwriting analysis, I hid my reaction. Could I actually be the more creative one? I changed the subject. "You know, we have to get back to the hotel to dress for dinner." Inside me was a storm. I felt competitive, excited, and guilty.

* * *

Several days later, while we were walking the streets of Paris, Claude peered into a fancy boutique. "I want to buy you a couture dress," he said. "Maybe a Chanel!" I became immediately overwhelmed.

"No, Claude, maybe next time," I said. I realized with his extravagant generosity, I was intimidated by the world he wanted me to enter. I didn't know how to behave in such a place, such an extremely refined world, especially dressed in Chanel. He couldn't understand my fears but was gentle with me. He did not judge me or make me self-conscious about my inability to acquire a fancy couture outfit.

"It's understandable," he said. "This is all new for you, we can go next time we are in Paris."

* * *

"Sara, wake up," Claude whispered in my ear.

"Why, what is happening?"

"We are going to the South of France to see my father. Today."

"But where will we stay?" I asked, shaking the sleep from my eyes.

"We can stay in Marie Chantal's mother's house in Ramatuelle. You'll like it. It's in a medieval village."

He didn't seem happy or excited, rather filled with trepidation. He knew that I was enthusiastic about meeting his father. Above all, he wanted to please me. We left Paris and drove in our new yellow Citroen car to St. Tropez. He had inherited some money from his great-grandmother, just before we left for France, and immediately bought a car when we arrived in Paris. Claude drove with his arms straight out to the steering wheel like a race-car driver and he took to the roads like a fugitive escaping prison, driving at speeds that would have meant an immediate arrest in America.

He decided that we would first visit his sister Maya, the daughter of Marie-Thérèse, Picasso's mistress from the 1930s. She was the only child from that union and lived in Marseille with her ship captain husband and two young sons. She looked exactly like Picasso except with blond hair and blue eyes. She was open and had a hearty laugh. Her husband was serious and quiet, with dark hair and a beard, and he took us to eat bouillabaisse on the wharf. The boys kept calling me mouchette, which means, "little fly." They thought it was funny that I spoke a different language.

Maya owned an extremely large painting by Picasso, which she proudly displayed in her dining room. It appeared so exotic in her simple home. She was more down-to-earth than the rest of the family and that made the appearance of the painting more dramatic.

The next day we left for Ramatuelle, a village built along the slant of the mountain. The house in which we stayed belonged to Marie Chantal's mother, who was Françoise Gilot's best friend. We had to park the car just outside the village and walk uphill to the house, a charming dwelling with rounded walls that seeemed to be on a slant. There were feral cats scattered about the hillside, and in the morning I fed them. They slinked around the curved pathways of the village, some gray, some white, and others calico. They were skittish when approached because the people who lived there did not like them. I walked up the street toward them while Claude watched me cautiously. I dropped some pieces of chicken near their path. They quickly grabbed the food and ran away.

"Sara!" he shouted. "Everyone will get angry with you feeding these cats. No one wants them around."

"But they still should be cared for," I said, throwing the last bits of chicken to the ground. I didn't care that they were stray and unwanted. They seemed hungry, and caring for them was something familiar to me. I felt at home. Cats were a great comfort to me, waiting for me when I came home from school and sleeping under the covers on my leg. These cats in this strange medieval village were familiar to me and gave me a comfort that I needed. I was also nervous about what would happen with Claude's father and whether he would reject my husband again.

We traveled around to different towns and one day we went through primeval-looking mountains and forests. I felt that we had driven into a fairy tale from a long time ago. Claude stopped the car and in the near distance we could see a mountain.

"Why are we stopping here?"

"Do you see that mountain?" Claude pointed to a peak rising in the distance. "That is called Mont Sainte-Victoire. My father bought that mountain." I leaned forward, twisting my neck so I could take in the entire vista. How does one buy a mountain?

"My father's hero was Cezanne. And this mountain was a subject of many of Cezanne's paintings. So he bought it."

"Oh my God," I exhaled as my eyes traced the lengthening slopes.

"Well, he also bought the shepherd and the sheep you see there," he said, pointing up. "And the castle." I gasped. Then I fell into gales of laughter at the absurd notion that Picasso owned everything on the mountain, even people and sheep. To think he needed to possess Cezanne's whole landscape to feel whole; it sounded fantastical. Suddenly the fairy tale was real. Claude's eyes darkened and he looked off.

There was no one around but I felt surrounded by wisps of unseen presences. I looked over at Claude, the son of the king of this castle.

"Claude, let's go inside. I would love to see more."

"No," he said nervously. "I am not allowed to go in there; it's best if we leave now." Suddenly he put the car in gear and we drove off, the castle disappearing in the sideview mirror.

CHAPTER 13

I couldn't understand why I couldn't enter the castle with my prince. We had come such an incredible distance to this remote mountainscape to meet his father, someone whose presence filled our daily encounters while in France. I dined under his paintings, I laughed with his daughter, and I listened to intimate stories of him as a father. I felt I was in a speeding car heading for my own personal encounter with this genius and yet Claude slammed the brakes on everything.

The next day, Claude wanted to show me Vallauris, the town in which Picasso did his pottery and where he lived with Françoise and Claude in a modest house in the center of the town. Françoise still owned the house and so we opened the front door and stepped back into his past. We went down a few steps to a room that was filled with his mother's paintings stacked against a wall. The house had molded plaster walls and small hobbit-like windows. Claude went over to a rolled-up poster and laid it open on the old farmhouse-style table. I recognized it immediately as a reproduction print of the famous Picasso painting from his blue period; it was of a man, woman, and a small boy, all of them with bowed heads. I saw that it was signed "To my son Claude, Pablo Picasso."

"Claude," I gasped, "this is a one-dollar poster, how could he give you a one-dollar poster?"

"I was away at school and he sent it to me," he said in a very matter-of-fact voice. My disbelief seemed to make him feel quietly distraught.

"But how could he send you a one-dollar poster?" His face sank. "Why would he do such an awful thing?" After a moment, Claude looked up.

"I don't know why," he conceded. His silence was an acceptance of the unfathomable: that his father did not care about him. My jaw fell, my mouth empty of words. There in front of me was material proof of Claude's pain: a cheap poster that I had seen so many times in my life, in so many stores. Now I was standing in a house that Picasso had lived in with Claude and his family and it all felt so twisted to me. This man who was so admired in the world was such an uncaring father. I couldn't quite believe what I was seeing and hearing.

"You know," Claude finally said, looking up with heavy eyes, "when I was fifteen my father told me, 'Why don't you become a garbage collector, it's a good profession.'" Claude's famous father, this genius of twentieth-century art, was like my brother, jealous and destructive with the son who loved him. I understood why at seventeen, the last time he had tried to see his father and didn't succeed, he had attempted to commit suicide. This was during his summer vacation and he had gone down to the South of France. He went to the house and was not allowed inside. He left the gate, walked around the house, and found a high wall overlooking the mountains of Cannes. He wanted to jump. After a moment he climbed down, deciding not to take his life.

After two or three days, we still had not made plans to see his father. I understand now, looking back, that Claude's hesitation was a reflection of his conflicted emotions about his father.

"Claude," I asked, "why haven't you called your father?"

"Not yet," he snapped. "I will call him soon."

Even though I was beginning to dislike his father, I was intensely curious about meeting him. I thought, rather naively, that once we got to Pablo's house, all would be healed. Why couldn't I tune in to his pain? His father's aura and the desire to be in the presence of his art overrode my care for Claude. I am not proud of that.

Then, on the fourth day, while we were having breakfast, Claude put down his fork.

"We are going today."

And with that, we gathered our things and off we drove to the hills above Cannes, to Mougins, where Pablo Picasso lived. Why Claude chose that moment, I am not sure. Maybe he gathered all his courage. Maybe his need to have a father who cared coupled with my naive belief that the meeting would go well pushed him to finally go.

We scaled the steep, winding hills until we reached a ledge of stone walls with a giant gate, like a fortress. I could not see the house, which was tucked within the clusters of cypress and olive trees surrounding the property. Claude got out of the car and walked up to the gate and spoke into the intercom.

"It is Claude," he announced timidly.

"Claude who?" a voice answered.

"Claude Picasso. I would like to see my father."

"Please wait," the voice instructed.

He stood there and after several minutes a car came up filled with what appeared to be workmen. It stopped and waited. After another few minutes a large man came walking down the hill; he looked at Claude through the bars of the gate.

"Your father is too busy to see you," he announced.

Then the gate opened and the car filled with workmen went through. As they passed Claude, they shouted, "You need a passport to get in here." They drove off through the gate, laughing.

He looked straight ahead at the truck flooded with construction workers as the gates closed behind them. Claude walked stiffly back to the car with his eyes downcast. We got in the car and began to drive down the hill. Waves of silence buried us both.

Then something happened to me, something that had never happened before: I could not speak for the next two hours. Claude, dejected and still, did not speak either. A part of me froze, but when I thawed I began to understand Claude's incredible pain. I understood why he didn't want to go to see his father. I also understood how unimportant his father's fame and creativity were compared to the hurt he had caused his son. My personal values would be forever changed.

We soon left Ramatuelle. Claude was visibly sad but stoic. I began to piece together all the stories that he had shared with me about his relationship with his father. I knew that Picasso was terrified of death and that Claude was sixty-five years younger than his father. For Picasso, this meant that his son would live much longer. I think that this caused tremendous jealousy in Picasso and as Claude grew older, his jealousy only increased. Picasso simply lacked the capacity to feel empathy for others. I'm not sure why Claude wanted us to visit his father and expose ourselves to rejection and cruelty. Maybe he was hoping that time and his new marriage would change things for the better. Sadly, he was wrong.

We drove farther south to the Camargue, an area with beaches, gypsies, and wild horses. It was January and the seaside towns felt desolate and mysterious. We stopped the car and entered a small stone church. Inside, there was a statue of a black gypsy saint named Sarah. The church was empty and lonely. I wondered whether I was his own Saint Sara, a protector who loved Claude for himself, not because he was Picasso's son. Claude shared stories of the gypsies with me and showed me the wild horses running on the beaches. He even began to smile again as he noticed how everything excited my interest.

CHAPTER 14

We decided to go back to Paris. I don't remember that we said very much about what had happened, because now there was a silent sadness between us. We saw his family again in Neuilly at his grandmother's home and they were slightly warmer and more accepting of me, but I was happy to be going back home to New York City.

Claude was so excited to be bringing his yellow Citroen to the United States. He said we would take the ship The France back to New York. We were also bringing back some small paintings of Picasso's and Françoise's. When we went through customs, the man asked Claude, "Who painted these works?" It was forbidden to take French works of art out of the country.

"They're just by my mother and father," Claude said.

"Fine," said the customs officer, and without looking at the names, he passed us through.

The ship was extravagant and huge. One afternoon,

I got lost and came upon a shoemaker! They even had a printing press on board. On our first night we had dinner at a very large table with the captain. He was a balding, white-haired man with a round face, a face that held both kindness and grace. The next morning we received an invitation to have dinner in his cabin.

The menus were printed with the names of all the guests at the dinner. We arrived to find Charles Matton and his girlfriend, Jeanine, seated at the table. With every course, and there were about six, we had a different liqueur or wine pairing. Everyone began to get tipsy. Charles Matton turned out to be a well-known painter in France and he revealed to me that he had seen me before we boarded the ship and said to himself, "She looks like a Picasso." He was stunned when he found out my last name. He was having his first exhibition of illustrations for Esquire magazine and he invited us to attend. Claude and I were so happy about this special evening and we went back to our cabin and made love, which we had not done since before our attempt to see his father.

The next morning, there was a knock on our cabin door, and a steward presented a thank-you note and a gift from the captain for me. It was a scarf with all the colors of the French flag in concentric circles—blue and red and white—and a book about the history of the ship. Our room was spacious and had two beds with gray-and-white striped wall covering, a desk, a chair, and a small bathroom. I sat down on the bed, holding my gifts while the ship gently rocked. I looked around my quarters, out the porthole to the open sea, and thought how just a few days ago I was not allowed to enter Claude's father's castle. Yet here, on The France, I was welcomed and treated so well. I knew that this was what I needed to heal my old family wounds as well. I promised myself to welcome this kindness throughout my life.

CHAPTER 15

I had my first experience of sea legs. After five days crossing the Atlantic, I felt wobbly when I exited down the gangplank. It took hours before I felt I was touching the ground. My parents were waiting at the dock with an insulated bag of food. My father could not stop smiling, a cheeriness pouring from his eyes. The massive ship, our new car here from across the ocean, it all intoxicated him. My mother was giggling and shy. Soon Claude's yellow Citroen came off the ship and we all packed the luggage securely in the trunk and drove to the new apartment on MacDougal Street.

A few weeks after we arrived home, we went to Charles Matton's opening for Esquire magazine and I bought one of his paintings. It was of a woman swimming in the ocean in Palm Beach with jewels around her neck and a swimming cap on her head, done in a cracked oil effect. Charles had never been to Palm Beach so it was his fantasy of the people who lived there. I paid one hundred dollars and it hangs in my home today. When I pass this painting in my hallway, I remember that this was the beginning of when I was able to trust myself.

With Claude's inheritance and a monthly stipend of four hundred dollars from his father, we began to buy lots of furniture to make our apartment a home. We bought a giant round maple wood table that seated twelve people and a small antique desk. Then Claude selected a modern white leather couch and an orange stereo component. I wanted to tell him I didn't like it, that it was ugly next to our antiques. But I said nothing. I trusted that his taste was superior to mine and that my design instincts were wrong.

Claude chose most of our furnishings because he had so much more knowledge about design. I could feel myself hesitate to tell him that I didn't like the orange stereo set that he bought or the Rauschenberg autobiographical prints. In this moment, I remembered the old handwriting expert who offered proof that I was creative. That analysis sent Claude reeling. The orange stereo set stayed. I said nothing.

Claude was hired by Vogue as a photographer and we began to have a life together, filled with friends and access to the upper echelons of New York society. Doors seemed to fly open and everyone wanted us at their dinners or parties. However, at home, Claude decided to teach me how to cook. I knew how to boil water for spaghetti but he made cooking exciting and creative. I became curious and loved how his coq au vin tasted. We had a tiny kitchen but this did not deter him: he mixed up eggs in a small bowl and added cheese and herbs and it arrived as an extraordinary omelet. This worldly young man knew more about the practicalities of living than a lower-middle-class girl from Brooklyn.

One day Claude came home with a new-style blender that also cooked hot food. He was more excited for this purchase than if he had nabbed a new photo job. I became infected with his enthusiasm and felt like we were making a home together. Neither of us were part of a family that celebrated everyday life and its simple joys, like blenders and omelets. We were both longing to re-create our idea of family.

Often, my mother would arrive at our door clutching her insulated bag full of food. Claude loved it. One day, when she was visiting, he suggested that we go visit my older brother, who lived on Long Island. In her forty-five years of marriage my mother never missed making dinner for my father at home. She jumped at the chance to have an adventure with Claude and off we went in the little yellow Citroen.

My father panicked when he returned home and could not find my mother. He called the police. Secretly, I was cheering that she had broken out of her shackles.

* * *

It was 1969 and the world was waking up to a time of experimentation and high energy. I was meeting people who wanted to sing in a new way, try drugs, throw off old roles, and be more sexually open. The rules were being challenged and I was getting more and more interested in all the excitement. The more I questioned the rules of society, the more withdrawn and grumpy Claude would become. This questioning and leaving definitions unclear, this exploring new ways of living, left him disturbed. He was a year and a half younger than I but he acted like someone from an older generation. This older quality made him very wise and gave me comfort and guidance, but it also made him seem less alive. When I first began to know Claude, I felt guided by him and his knowledge of a world that was unknown to me, but now the restrictions were becomig suffocating.

On our first Christmas together, I trimmed my very first Christmas tree and handcrafted my own Christmas cards. There was a wonderful paper shop that sold paper in luscious colors and textures along with unique ornaments for the Christmas tree. I bought stacks of papers and picked out my first Christmas ornaments, some paper cats and colorful tin Mexican angels. With my bag of supplies, I began assembling the cards as Claude looked over my shoulder and said, in a flat voice colored with some jealousy, "They look nice."

We purchased a large Christmas tree that I decorated like a child clothing her first doll. We invited friends and gave them each a special present. At last, I could have a holiday celebration! I tried to make every detail perfect. I went out and bought an antique child's puzzle to give as a gift to one of the women. It wasn't large but it had faded colors from another time. I liked that it was old and that it had a history. That first Christmas together uncovered a strong desire for festive rituals in my life and gave me a sense of place in my own newly shaped history.

Claude and I were so young and trying to be more mature than we really were. At first, we spent a great deal of time with older people, friends who were more established in the world. The Rosenthals were of course our godparents, always taking us under their wings, treating us to dinner and buying us many gifts. We were also friendly with Richard Kasack and his wife, Harriet. He owned a successful group of bookstores called Bookmasters. Claude had two photographers whom he liked—Ryszard Horowitz and Gianfranco Gorgoni. Gorgoni was a tough Italian street kid credited with being an amazing survivor. Horowitz went on to become a famous surrealist photographer. He was also a survivor, the youngest survivor of Auschwitz, five years old when he left the camps.

During our first year of marriage, I traveled with Richard and Harriet Kasack to Mexico. Claude arrived later and when we went to pick him up at the airport, we noticed he wasn't coming through customs. We saw Claude arguing with the officials: "What are you, stupid," he bellowed, "I have a visa! Just look, I have a green card! You are ridiculous!" I ran over and said, "Claude, please calm down, stop insulting them." I began to plead with the officials: "Please! This is my husband, we have small children and you must let him in, he'll apologize to you." He did so rather reluctantly. I could see the steam coming out of his head but he remained silent. And so, he entered Mexico. I was seeing the cracks in his personality, a deep insecurity that enveloped us in a strong negative energy.

In Mexico, we went to the ruins and I met my classmate from the fifth grade! Harriet was so annoyed because I was always meeting people wherever we would go. She seemed threatened by my enthusiasm. She was uptight and judgmental and, like many of the woman in our circle, wanted all of Claude's attention. Like my mother, I was naive about certain things, such as the impact of Claude's fame on other people, especially women. But I was indeed getting a fast education. One night, the Kasacks, Claude, and I went to a restaurant in an old hacienda. It was the largest house I had ever been in. I leaned over to Claude and said, "Can you imagine living in a house like this one?" He turned to me and said, "Yes, I can. I have." As if struck by a thunderbolt, I began to understand, not in my head but in my entire body, how different our lives had been.

CHAPTER 16

A check arrived every month for Claude signed by Pablo Picasso. The check usually covered our rent and basic living expenses. For most of his life, Claude was not legally recognized as Pablo Picasso's son. When he was young, his mother began a legal battle to get the French government to give him legal status as a legitimate son of Picasso. His parents were never married and as a "love child" he was not entitled to that name. His mother knew that she must get him the name Picasso for him to be legally recognized as Pablo Picasso's son and therefore an heir to Picasso's estate. She enlisted many powerful people to help her and she succeeded. So, when he was about twelve years old, he and his sister Paloma had their names changed to Ruiz-Picasso.

He then began to receive this monthly allowance from his father. He earned money as a photographer and I earned a little money as an actress. I met an agent and he sent me out on my first film audition for a director named Barry Brown who was making his first feature film, The Way We Live Now. I was cast in a small part as an English secretary. I've never forgotten my line: "Mr. Aldridge, Mr. Aldridge, the AMX shooting is taking place." I had an upper-class English accent. I also got my Screen Actors Guild card. My dream of becoming a working actress was taking shape. Before this happened, I was feeling afraid to push myself and go to auditions; I wasn't sure that I was a good enough actress to actually get work.

The next film I did was A Safe Place, with Tuesday Weld and Orson Welles, directed by Henry Jaglom. I was told to go to the boat pond in Central Park. I had no idea about the specifics of my character or what the scene was about, it was a new kind of improvising in film. Sitting at a table by the lake was Tuesday Weld and a girl from my high school, Margo. I remembered seeing Margo every day in high school. She would be in the bathroom, standing in front of the full-length mirror, taking up all the space. Like Narcissus looking into the pond, Margo was combing her long, blond hair, gazing at her reflection. Later in the day, I spent a few hours in a rowboat in the pond with Tuesday Weld, who was sweet and gentle.

I felt drawn to fame and wanted to be around famous people. I was raised to imagine that I could be one of them—not just a princess for a day, but a princess every day. Yet, I was beginning to feel, within the first year of my marriage to Claude, that there were a lot of rules I was expected to follow. Claude insisted that we see only our older friends and one or two of his photographer buddies.

I was not allowed to smoke marijuana and he was weary of all the new ideas of the 1960s. We were surrounded by political and cultural upheaval and in response Claude became more conservative. My desire to rebel began to take seed. I was too curious about the world and myself to be kept so restricted. I began to explore what kind of woman I truly wanted to be. I wanted to make more of my own choices.

* * *

I became friendly with a crazy actress named Jesse, who might have slept with everyone in the Village, living out her 1960s credo. She knew many artists, from jazz musicians to celebrities in the art world. I also became friends with Jan McGuire, a Ford model whom Claude would regularly photograph. She lived on Gramercy Park with four other models, and all of these new friends were going out, experimenting with all new freedoms that were in the air. I was twenty-four and wanted to have a life with greater openness to these exciting freedoms. I didn't have much responsibility and would spend afternoons hanging out with Jan, who loved to laugh. She was from the South and had grown up all around the world. Jesse felt more like a mother figure to me. I was feeling lost and confused. I thought that I should feel so lucky to have so much in my life, but I didn't feel happy and I didn't know why. Jesse, on the other hand, seemed so sure of things. Claude had been my teacher and now I was looking for a new guide, one who could supply me with quick and simple solutions. I was bored with my life with Claude and I felt guilty about these feelings. So I let Jesse feed me answers to my questions. This exercise turned out to be a dangerous choice.

One night, on our way home from a party, Jesse, Claude, and I stopped at a red light in our yellow Citroen. A taxi pulled up next to us and the handsome driver with green eyes and a cleft in his chin waved to Jane. As we pulled away, I remember trying to catch another glimpse of him through our back window. Those green eyes, the cleft in his chin—I was instantly attracted to him.

"Jesse," I asked, trying to be casual, "who was that?"

"Oh, that's my friend Douglas," she replied, "an out-of-work actor."

The next day when Jesse and I were alone, I asked her whether we could see him again. "I could arrange that," she said, her lips widening into a coy smile. She and I were beginning to sabotage my marriage.

When I awoke a few days later, the light seemed crisp and warm coming through the window. I thought of Douglas and my stomach flipped. I felt a surge of energy rush through my body as I slipped into one of my favorite dresses, the one that delicately clung to my body. I chose a pair of dangling turquoise earrings that seemed to gently kiss my neck as they swayed within my blond ringlets. When I arrived at Jesse's apartment, she had a smile on her face when she opened the door, the wicked grin of a Cheshire cat. We buzzed with giddy excitement and anticipation as we waited for Douglas to arrive. Finally, we heard a knock. When Jesse opened the door, Douglas towered in the entrance. I instantly fell into his rich green eyes, which had a distinctive Irish twinkle. He had broad shoulders and strong, capable hands— he seemed to exude sex. We could not stop looking at each other. After we had some wine, he took me aside and asked for my phone number. I felt something leap within me, thrilling and dangerous at the same time. I fantasized about entering his apartment, falling into his kisses, and hearing him tell me how much he wanted me.

At home, my sexual life with Claude had become routine. Our intimacy, the thrill of exploring each other's bodies, talking into the night—these things seemed erased from our marriage. It seemed Claude and I were at a fork in the road and I took the open, sunny path while he disappeared into the dark forest. My path was filled with curiosities, vibrant color, a new and bright music, sensual drugs, and sexual freedom. His forest hid land mines for me.

As the days progressed, Claude grew more morose and withdrawn. He had little desire to go out into the world. He didn't want to see any of my friends but sought the company of our older friends, those who were our parental figures. His own parental figures were so distant and removed; he longed for real, nurturing parents. So he found substitutes. We were no longer orbiting the same sun; our planets were diverging.

He detested my new friends. One couple, Herbert

and Renny, were glamorous and adventurous, always open to new ideas and experiences, and loved to have parties. Herbert owned a financial company and Renny was interested in the arts. I became very fond of their chauffeur, Hayward, a wise soul who resembled Yoda. Hayward was a free spirit who lived by no rules, except one: kindness to all. Hayward came to every party and Herbert would seek his advice about everything from business to love. I took an instant liking to Hayward and forged a friendship with him, which seemed to infuriate Claude. After all, Hayward was "only" a chauffeur and this career choice made Claude quite uncomfortable.

"These people aren't interesting!" he insisted. "Why are you hanging out with a chauffeur?"

"They are interesting to me," I told him. "Hayward is one of the wisest men I've ever met."

"Sara," he quickly snapped, "this guy Herbert must be crazy, getting advice about his life from his chauffeur." The strange irony was that Claude's brother Paulo had been his father's chauffeur. I couldn't tell whether Claude had repressed his brother's history or that memory fueled his dislike of Hayward. His quick judgment gave him tunnel vision and stopped him from seeing the value in the person inside the uniform and cap.

One night, Claude and I had a party at our apartment, which attracted quite the large crowd. People were smoking joints and drinking sake. Crosby, Stills, Nash and Young played on an endless loop on our orange stereo set. Claude seemed to withdraw from the entire party. I caught a glimpse of him sitting alone in our study, looking out the window at our backyard. I wished he would just leave me to be young, laughing, and dancing freely with my friends. He was horrified that the chauffeur was sitting at our dining table, rolling joints and partying with this group of elite artist friends and socialites. I remember when Claude told his mother of our engagement, she warned him that I was not of his class, which would be a problem. Now he was reacting the same way to Hayward. I hated his attitude and dismissal of someone because of his job and economic status. I hated that he couldn't see Hayward as a person with heart and thoughts and value. Claude was embodying the same prejudices of his disapproving mother. I didn't care about his glum restrictions. I was on my way to breaking free of the chains of our marriage. I still loved him but I did not love the life that he was demanding that I live.

Douglas called me the next day. I rushed into the next room so that Claude wouldn't hear our conversation. I was frightened by the secrecy of my longing for Douglas, but couldn't contain my excitement at the thought of a rendezvous at his tiny apartment in the East Village. "Claude, I'm running out to see my friend Jan," I called behind me. "I'll see you later." At a pay phone on my way to the East Village, I called Jan to cover for me without telling her why.

I found Douglas's apartment and knocked on the door. He answered with a big smile on his face. Walking in, I realized it was a tiny studio apartment and I found myself right by his bed. As soon as Douglas took off my coat, he began to unbutton my blouse and didn't stop running kisses all over my neck. His hands quickly found my breasts and he began to kiss them. I was captive to his expert control and his steady advance down my body. He slid his hands down my hips, under my panties, and slowly moved his fingers gently inside me. I felt his small room vanish and I disappeared into the world he and I were creating. When he was done, my whole body was shaking and coming alive. I never knew that sex could be like this and I instantly became addicted. On our second encounter, he had me sniff a popper, which blocked the outside world completely so that all I could feel was his touch on my body.

I learned that Douglas was having a long affair with an older actress whose husband was a well-known director. He really loved her and was very comfortable with married women who didn't want too much from him. It was a relief for me to be with someone like Douglas, a man who had little status and just accepted me as I was.

Meanwhile, I was still a part of Claude's lavish social life. We were once invited to the home of the record mogul Ahmet Ertegun, the owner of Atlantic Records, and his socialite wife, the interior designer Mica Ertegun, for a dinner honoring Crosby, Stills, Nash and Young. We were welcomed into the luxurious dining room filled with ornately dressed tables and walls lined with original Magrittes, Rauschenbergs, and a host of other well-known artists. I had never seen this kind of art collection except in a museum. I found myself asking, Where do I fit in? When will I feel like I have earned my place among the rich and famous? Will I ever feel accomplished? There was Sara Lee Schultz, there was Sara Picasso, and then there was a Sara whose name I didn't yet know. I had a drive and energy that I hadn't fully tapped into yet and that made me lethargic and sad. Where was the girl who liked to outrun all the boys on the block when she was ten years old? Where was she? I wanted to find her and tell her that I was her friend.

I pictured Douglas and his tiny studio apartment, how he opened up something inside me. There were Jesse and Hayward and all the parties, the drugs, and the rhythms, which captivated me more than the stuffiness of Claude's more controlled and quieter world. I realized I was astride two lives: my domestic life with Claude, which was slowly withering away, and the promise of a new life filled with sexual experimentation and a new freedom. I regretted lying to Claude about my affair with Douglas because I knew I would hurt him, but nevertheless, I felt I had no choice but to breathe in this sexual side of me. Claude had been betrayed by his family, and now by his wife. The more I felt Claude imposing his reign over me, the more I ran to be with Douglas.

One warm summer day, Douglas decided to walk me home for the first time. One of Claude's best friends, Jean Franco, was on the street and saw Douglas with his arm around me. I looked at Jean, he looked at me, and without a word he turned and walked away. That was the beginning of the end.

During this time, I had a blouse put away at Betsey Bunky Nini, the chicest young dress shop at the time. One of the shopgirls said to her manager, "Oh, I wanted that blouse!" The manager replied, "That's for Sara Picasso." The girl said, "Who is Sara Picasso?!"

A few days later, I came to pick up my blouse. I noticed a friend from high school named Noelle, who was talking to one of the girls who worked at the shop. Noelle introduced me to Marci and she turned out to be the girl who wanted my blouse. They invited me to join them for lunch. I listened carefully to Marci giving Noelle advice and I realized that she was quite brilliant and special. We lived near each other in Greenwich Village and a few days later I called her for lunch. We sat in an old Revolutionary War garden behind her small basement apartment. That was the beginning of a close friendship that has lasted for over forty years.

Marci and I began to spend more time together. She let me read her writing. I realized that she was a talented writer and I began to encourage that part of her, which had been dormant while living with her cruel second husband. We smoked grass together and talked about Anaïs Nin. We both were longing to fly away from our lives.

Claude called her Merci Beaucoup. One day during dinner, Claude and Marci got into a discussion about personal freedom and self-definition.

"We are all persons of our own inventions, Claude," Marci said, "we make our existence, we can self-create, we can do whatever we want with our lives." Claude grimaced.

"I can't do what you are doing," he said. "Do you know who my father is?"

"Yes, I know," Marci said, letting out a sigh, "but he's just a father. My father was a postman and he's just a father. My issues with my father are the same as your issues with your father." Claude looked dismayed. After a pause he looked up.

"But my father is Picasso." At that moment it seemed like a screen was lowered, a barrier slicing between us, and Claude was no longer in the room. He was not going to sit quietly and be identified as just another hurt son of a rejecting father. Marci had crossed a line.

I was watching him during this conversation, noticing how stiff his body appeared. I saw anger building up behind a frozen stare. Marci was speaking from her heart, providing great insight and trying to connect with Claude about this very sensitive subject. He was resisting connecting to his deeper and more introspective self. He was threatened by the idea that he was just another son with father issues. Even though he had been deeply scarred by this man, he needed the role of "the son of Picasso" as some sort of protection, a buffer between his feelings and the world. When he protested Marci with such vigor, I felt a wave sending me farther out to sea, away from him.

CHAPTER 17

One night when I was wracked with guilt, I confided to Jesse. "You have to tell Claude about Douglas," she said. "The truth will bring you two closer." I wanted to believe her.

Back at home, Claude and I had been fighting about the differences in the ways we wanted to live. "Smoking grass is something I did a long time ago," he chided, "I'm over it now!"

"You are so angry and judgmental!" I snapped. "You have so little enthusiasm for life."

"These friends are a waste of your time. The way you are acting is so immature."

"That's it!" I finally shouted. "I'm tired of your criticisms and restrictions." Silently, he walked out of the room and I felt an ocean rise between us, getting larger and with no land in sight.

A few weeks later, when I was visiting his photography studio, which I would do sometimes to see what he was working on, we tried to discuss our differences. He looked at me with calm eyes. "You know the student always leaves the teacher." His demeanor was surprisingly calm. It seemed we had reached a peaceful acknowledgment. He was finally being respectful of my right to find my own way.

I decided that I could no longer contain my guilt over being with Douglas. Claude and I were in our dining room, standing across from each other, the large table between us. He was getting his cameras ready for a shoot the next day, I was going through some paperwork, my hands busy with the pile of bills. There was a silence between us, something in the room that neither of us wanted to talk about. I put down my papers and looked up at him. He caught me staring and put his camera down. I breathed for a moment and looked away. Then I slowly began to speak: "I'm having an affair with a man named Douglas." He looked down, shaking his head, muttering, "No, no." Then he slowly walked away from me, pacing along the wall. I stood still, waiting for some big reaction, the volcano erupting, the bomb going off. He breathed heavily. Suddenly he raised his arm and punched his fist through the wall. I stared for a moment into the jagged hole he left in the wall. Then he ran out of the house. I followed him, screaming to him, "Please let me talk to you! Claude! Please stop running!" He ran into the subway station, darting in and out of the parked train as I desperately tried to stop him. I was out of breath, tears streaming down my face. Then he stopped running and I caught up to him. We stood on the platform, trying to catch our breath. Without a word he inhaled deeply and walked out of the station. I followed him until we reached home.

The next few days blurred together in slow motion. The air in the house was thick with silence. I knew there was little I could say except to apologize. "I can't tell you enough how terrible I feel to have hurt you so much." Claude would not look at me. "I felt strangled by you and I needed to break free." Somewhere I felt the courage to continue. "I know I have no right to ask for your understanding but I want to try and fix our marriage, can we go for help?" After a long silence he raised his head, slowly exhaled, and said, "I don't know what I want to do."

A few days later, Claude came home with a Felix the Cat wall clock. It was sparkly black and had a tail that rocked back and forth with the movement of time. He went to the closet and got a hammer and a nail. He walked into the dining room, not saying a word, and approached the hole he had left in the wall. When the nail was in place, he hung the cat clock on the wall, the narrow body barely covering the hole.

In an attempt to regain some sanity at home, Claude and I acted as if everything was okay. A few days later, as I was feeding our cat, Claude came into the room. "Sara," he said, looking directly into my eyes, "I am going on a trip."

"When will you be back?" I asked.

"I will return in a month," he said, "but I need time to think about what I want to do."

Then he was gone. The house was empty. Every week, a postcard from a different city arrived in our mailbox with no message, just "Claude" signed on the back and underlined. He never lived with me again.

PART IV

After Claude

CHAPTER 18

While Claude was away, I felt a surge of energy and a desire to try new things. I joined an acting workshop at Café La MaMa, the experimental theater in the East Village. My interest in the sexual experimentation in the East Village had waned as soon as I told Claude about my affair. One day at the entrance to the La MaMa theater I saw a beautiful young Japanese man going through a door. I asked the person at the box office who he was and learned he was part of the Japanese troupe the Tokyo Kid Brothers, who were having auditions for a new work, not yet formed or titled. I opened the same door and followed him up the stairs. I entered a room filled with Japanese people auditioning white actors. A small, wiry man was seated at the center of the room and asked me in halting English whether I wanted to audition for their new play. I said yes, of course. I sat down on the floor and waited my turn to audition, and that was the beginning of my new life.

The troupe had been performing a play called Golden

Bat at an off-Broadway theater on Sheridan Square. They were very successful. We began to create this new play that would combine American and Japanese actors who could hardly communicate with one another. Everyone involved was young, enthusiastic, and open to everything we attempted to create. It was September 1970 in America.

The process of creating what became The Coney Island Play was filled with true excitement. It was being written as we improvised with one another and we all tried to communicate with little knowledge of one another's language or culture. One scene that emerged took place with two actors on either side of the stage. The American actor would whisper a curse word in the Japanese actor's ear and he would scream it at the other Japanese actor. This interaction went on back and forth for about five minutes and became more and more hilarious as each tried to pronounce fuck, shit, schmuck, bastard, and the like.

Working with the troupe was open and free, the opposite of my restricted life with Claude. I hardly understood what the members of the troupe were saying but I learned about the differences between the American and Japanese way of thinking. I remembered the geta my brother had sent to me from Japan when I was ten years old. I had always wanted to know more about the exotic land where these bright red platform shoes had originated.

Every day felt like a wonderful adventure. I flirted

with one of the actors whose face was chiseled like an American Indian chief's. I thought that I was falling in love with the director, Mr. Higashi. He was so intense and unpredictable. Yet, I was having very strong feelings toward the composer of the troupe, Itsuro Shimoda. He was six feet tall, with long, black hair that hit his shoulders, and his face was like carved rock. He was also married. We began to secretly hide away at any moment we could. When we made love, his skin was the most sensual thing I had ever touched—softness and toughness combined. He had no hair on his body so it felt like being with a man and a woman at the same time. Yet, Itsuro had macho Japanese attitudes, such as requiring me, the woman, to walk behind him, the man. He wrote beautiful melodies and sang them while playing his guitar. Although he walked like a mighty samurai, he sang like a nightingale. I had fallen madly in love with my Japanese lover. No one in the troupe knew about us. I guess I liked keeping secrets.

We would have parties at my home with everyone from all of my worlds combined. It was 1970 and we felt that this was a time to enjoy life, a new frontier. I continued to get a postcard from Claude every week. Because of this new freedom, I was creating my own world and that world felt like the most important thing at this time in my life.

We performed The Coney Island Play at Café La MaMa in the fall of 1970 and Clive Barnes from the New York Times gave us a wonderful review. Claude came back to New York, but not to our home. He called me and said he wanted to see the play, but that he was living with friends. After seeing the play, we walked together in the street. He was quiet. "I didn't like the play," he blurted. I was hurt by his flippant criticism. Then he stopped and looked into my eyes, "I now know that your allegiance is somewhere else." He left me standing on the street corner as I tried to avoid the harsh light from the streetlamp.

A few days later I received a call from Claude, asking me to meet him at the office of Raoul Felder, the divorce lawyer to the stars. On the phone he sounded distant yet urgent. "Sara," he said, "I want you to meet me at my lawyer's office on Tuesday, can you do that?"

"Yes, I will be there, what is the address and the time?" I was extremely naive about lawyers and went there without a speck of knowledge about what to do. I believed whatever they told me and so they proceeded to arrange for me to be represented by a lawyer named Martin Wright. Boy, did he turn out to be Martin Wrong.

They quickly arranged for me to sign a divorce agreement, which I did. At this time, I needed to leave for Japan and quickly found someone to take care of my cats. The Rosenthals stored my Robert Rauschenberg prints and a Saul Steinberg print inscribed with Saul's iconic gibberish. All of my other possessions I left in the apartment. Claude came by one day to take back some small paintings done by his father. I gave back all the paintings. I took off the silver medallion that Picasso had etched with a portrait of Claude as a child and threw it in the bag. It was my favorite piece of jewelry, but he had asked me to return all the gifts he had given me. When I tried to give him back the silver cup that his father had etched with Claude's name, he refused. Nor did he accept the vibrant blue pastel painting that Luc Simon, his ex-stepfather, had painted of him as a ten-year-old boy at his typewriter. He took everything else, dumped everything in a black plastic bag, and closed the door behind him. Immediately, the door opened again. Claude stared at me, his face contorted with sadness, anger, and regret. Then there seemed a softening of his brow, a dim light of love in his eyes. After ten long seconds, he closed the door again. The door stayed closed for many years.

CHAPTER 19

"Why in the world did you give everything back?" Marci asked one day at lunch.

"Well, he may never have anything else from his father and I would feel terrible about that." Marci looked utterly perplexed.

"Sara, he has his father's name and he will inherit a great deal of paintings and money someday. Don't you realize that?"

I guess I did not. Since that time many people have been shocked that I returned everything. Most were actually horrified. I was naïve about how the world worked, but I felt most strongly that I wanted to be free of the world that I inhabited with Claude and free of the heavy burden that those artworks represented. I wanted the unknown, no matter how scary it might be. I didn't realize at that time how scary it could be, but I would find out.

I arranged for two members of the Japanese troupe

to live in my apartment and take care of our cats; I sold some other things, and within a month I left for Tokyo to join the Tokyo Kid Brothers for a new performance and to live on a very different stage.

I arrived at Narita Airport in Tokyo after a fourteen-hour flight on New Year's Eve 1971. I was met by the Tokyo Kid Brothers' entire troupe, about fifteen people. They were all laughing and smiling and speaking to me in Japanese and broken English. They told me they were going to take me to the Meiji Shrine in the middle of Tokyo, a place where many Japanese go on the dawn of the New Year to make a wish.

We drove back to Tokyo from the airport to their office. As we made our way to the Meiji Shrine, I looked around and realized that everyone was Japanese. For the first time in my life, I was the only Caucasian person. I was in a place where everyone was the same race, religion, and origin. They all had black hair and dark almond eyes. I felt I had landed in the middle of one big family. I felt very self-conscious of my blond curly mop of hair, white skin, and blue eyes. There were hundreds of thousands of people and we were all being pushed along into a stream of humanity that I had never experienced the likes of before. I wasn't afraid, just mesmerized by how this setting was different from all that I had known. During our marriage, Claude had taken a trip to Japan. When he returned he introduced me to Japanese food. Little did I know then that I was the one who would soon call Japan my home.

After going to the Shrine, we went back to the Tokyo Kid Brothers office in an area of Tokyo called Shibuya. We sat around and then someone suggested that we go eat and drink sake. I left my luggage because it appeared that I would be sleeping temporarily at the office; it seemed everyone was quite loose about how things were done. Shimoda was there with his wife and I was excited to see him but could not reveal my feelings.

During the next few days we began to rehearse the new play. We were scheduled to perform in a month. We rehearsed in an old schoolhouse and I had a small scene with a Japanese actress named Kayoko. We would speak Japanese and English together. After the second day of rehearsals, one of the members put me in a taxicab and said I should go back to the office; everyone else stayed at rehearsals. They understood that my lack of knowledge in Japanese would not let me participate in the rehearsal. The taxi doors close automatically in Japan, and I was completely terrified about what would happen next, knowing no Japanese and not having a clue as to where the office was. There are only street names for the large avenues in Japan. Behind the large streets, there are little villages with no street names and you have to tell a cabdriver, "It is near there, next to that." But I couldn't communicate any of that, so when the cab came to a sudden stop and I got out, I took a deep, deep breath. Lucky for me, I have a photographic memory of places. I looked around and I began to walk through the labyrinth of tiny streets until I found the office.

Beginning the next day, I started to learn some Japanese. I could navigate and feel some sense of control in this new environment. The strangest thing was that even though so much of it was alien and different, I felt comfortable. I loved the way everyone looked, the beautiful thick black hair and full eyebrows, the generally sleek bodies, the openness on their faces when I spoke to them. I loved all the food. Because I could eat natto (special fermented soybeans), which most foreigners didn't attempt to try, they called me a henna gaijen, strange foreigner. Everyone who is not Japanese is a gaijen.

After a few more days of rehearsals and staying at the office, Shimoda asked me to go drinking with him. There used to be little streets lined with drinking places behind shoji screens that could fit maybe ten people. There was always an older woman cooking little delicious dishes of fish and vegetables and serving bottles of hot sake. He took me to one of these places and we began to drink. I have never been a big drinker but that night I had five bottles of sake and there is one hour of my life that I don't remember. The next morning I woke up and realized that we were living together. He told me that he had left his wife and would now live with me. A few nights later we had to go to a restaurant in a department store and meet his father, his wife, and her sister and make this formal declaration. I did not understand a word that was spoken. His wife seemed to take the whole thing in stride, but then again she was Japanese and trained to restrain certain emotions while in public. I felt badly for her but the whole event seemed oddly natural.

One day, Shimoda took me to a pink hotel and we stayed the night. It was in the middle of a street and he told me that people go there to have sex for one hour or one day, however long they want to stay. I was nervous that it would be a tacky and unclean place but it was the opposite. We were shown into a very clean room with tatami on the floor and sat cross-legged by a low chestnut wood table. A lady in a Kimono served us tea, gracious and quiet. I was wondering where the bed was when she quietly slid back a shoji-screened door and revealed a futon on the floor; then she left. It was all so calm and quiet. There was a minor earthquake in Tokyo at the time; unaware of this fact, I just thought things were intense between us. When we left the hotel the next morning, a man stopped and took a photograph of us. I guess he liked the way we looked together.

We lived together in Shibuya in one room with tatami on the floor. In the middle of the room was a table and around the table was heating built into the floor, so we would sit on the floor and put our feet down under the table to keep warm. It is not as cold in Tokyo in the winter as in New York, but it is not warm either. Shimoda would cook Japanese food for us, lots of rice and noodles, and for breakfast we would have fish and rice and miso soup. We started our day with a full meal as though it were lunch or dinner. During the day we would go to rehearsals, where we felt totally accepted. I struggled with feeling guilty about his wife but he kept reassuring me that he didn't love her.

I loved exploring Tokyo by myself. I would walk along the streets and find amazingly delicious and exotic things to eat for twenty-five cents. It wasn't so long after the war and Japan was still inexpensive. There were few foreigners who lived in Tokyo, but everyone was so polite and people would never stare at me. At night, Shimoda and I would go to drink sake at the same tiny shop run by the old woman where I once drank five bottles of the potent beverage. I have never drunk that much before or since. There were always vegetables and fish that would be served alongside of the sake and they were always delicious. We made love once or twice a day.

After two months, Marci decided to come on a buying trip to Tokyo. We picked her up at the airport and as the car traveled the highway to Tokyo, she turned and told me that she felt the surroundings were familiar to her.

"But I have to go back to my husband," she said.

"You are never going back to him," I replied, knowing she was in an abusive relationship and she needed to change her life. Marci slept on a futon next to our bed for four weeks. We felt like explorers wanting to try everything. She became involved with a designer named Kansai Yamamoto. They were a funny pair: he was tall and bald with a big personality, dressed in wild, colorful clothes. Marci was tiny, dressed in clean black lines, and reserved. I was happy that she had a boyfriend. But we had plans to travel and she would have to leave him.

Shimoda, Marci, and I decided that we wanted to

travel to Europe together. While we were in Sweden, I missed my period. I was frightened that I might be pregnant. I thought of all the sake I drank in Japan and I began to panic. Through my crisis, Shimoda was distant, yet Marci was there, holding my hand. I went to a Swedish doctor and he told me, "Go to Poland immediately." In Poland, I could get a cheap abortion. Poland was a Communist country at the time and I knew there was a strong possibility that I would never return. I knew that this was not the time in my life that I could be a good mother and I knew that Shimoda was not the man to be the father of my child. I wanted the father of my child to be a caring and trustworthy person and not someone as self-involved as Shimoda. But it was still painful to make the decision to give up a child. I went back and forth in my mind about how I could take care of the child and realized that I was completely and totally unprepared to provide it a good life. I was still legally married to Claude. I knew what I had to do.

I had to convince the Swedish government that I needed an abortion. I was determined that they would grant me permission to have the procedure in a Swedish hospital. I had to meet with an official of the government because I was a foreigner. Nervously, I entered his neat office and sat down across from him. He had a large, dark wood desk with nothing out of place. Without a hesitation his first question pierced the silence: "Why do you need this abortion?" I didn't know what to say. "You are already almost three months pregnant," he continued. I paused to collect my thoughts. I felt far away from everything comfortable.

"The father of my baby is in Japan and I will never see him again." The official looked unsympathetic. I continued, "He is not a good man and I cannot afford to raise this child by myself." He stared at me with his piercing blue eyes, and I immediately felt exposed. Then, without looking at me, he announced, "All right, you will go to one of our hospitals. You are not a Swedish citizen, so the procedure will cost you five hundred dollars." He handed me a piece of paper.

"Thank you," I said quietly, my heart thumping. As I exited the office, I began to panic about how I was going to get five hundred dollars. I rushed back to Marci and Shimoda to tell them. After we talked about each possibility, I decided to call a young, wealthy art dealer I knew in New York and sell him my oak dining table. He bought it for five hundred dollars and I had the abortion.

When it was done, we decided that we needed a complete change. We got very cheap tickets to the island of Majorca, off the coast of Spain. At the hotel we met an odd guy who took us to a house outside of the main city of Palma. It was a real hacienda with a field of almond trees behind the house. Blue and white tiles adorned the floors and wooden beams ran the length of the ceiling. There was a huge terrace where we could eat. The first night we went out onto the terrace, we heard the most hauntingly beautiful sounds. The goats were allowed into the fields from neighboring farms; they wore bells around their bare necks. As they moved among the trees, the bells created a symphony in the still night air. Instead of traffic and horns and sirens, I found the sounds of a Majorca night easing my weary traveler's soul.

On the farm, the twisted trunks of the almond trees rose from a vibrant orange earth. Marci and I cooked while Shimoda played his guitar. After dinner, Marci wrote, and I took out my pencils and sketchbook. We hitchhiked every day along a narrow winding road bordered by old stone walls. We felt free as the breezes that flowed through Can Arbona, the exotic name of our new home. It was 1971 and we shaved our eyebrows and declared ourselves "elite hippies."

Having very little money left, we began to get hungry. Shimoda came up with the idea of painting Japanese dragons on T-shirts to sell to the American navy. Their giant aircraft carrier was docked in Palma. Shimoda drew the first dragons and we followed. We went to town with all our T-shirts and began selling them to the sailors. They invited us on the ship and we instructed them, "Just wash them in cold water so the colors won't run." We used tempera paint on the cotton; the colors would run no matter what they washed them in. But we got to eat lots of rice.

After three months, we wanted to get back to New York. Marci and Shimoda had written many songs that we thought we could turn into a show and perform at Café La MaMa. The same strange man got us cheap airplane tickets from Paris to New York, but first we had to take a boat, a bus, and finally a train to reach Paris.

I knew from my last conversation with Claude that he had returned to Paris, so when we arrived there, I called him and told him that we were seriously hungry. I asked whether he would take us to dinner. I wanted to go to this special place near Notre Dame. This was the definition of the Yiddish word chutzpah. He was obviously upset and said, "I don't want to take them to dinner! I just want to take you to dinner alone."

"No," I protested, "you have to take all of us, we're starving and we haven't eaten anything in two days." Finally, he gave in and we hurried to the restaurant to eat everything in sight. I then spent the night with Claude in the attic of the house in Neuilly under Picasso's portrait of Françoise Gilot as a flower.

While lying in bed with my estranged husband, I was completely unaware of how he was feeling. I was an enfant terrible when I was with him—just communicating my needs without considering his own feelings. When we parted that morning, after he took me back to Shimoda and Marci, I felt a lingering sadness. I knew my marriage to him was over. As we hauled our luggage to the airport, I felt a new life was waiting for me in New York.

CHAPTER 20

Back in New York, Shimoda and I moved into a loft in SoHo. One day when I came home from an acting job, Shimoda told me that Hollywood had called. "Oh, come on," I said, "who from Hollywood is calling me?"

"Francis Ford Coppola," he answered. "He wants to speak to you."

Years before, I had auditioned for Francis at the St. Regis Hotel, back when I was first married to Claude. He had written a script and the part called for a girl to be smoking a marijuana joint. I rolled a small joint and brought it to the audition and lit it up. He was very surprised. I was excited by the news and called him back. He got on the phone right away after his secretary said Sara Picasso was returning his call.

"I'll be in New York next week and I would love to see you, can you meet me for dinner?" I quickly answered, "Yes, of course."

He took me to a Japanese restaurant in the Village. Energy spouted out of him, filling the room as he told me stories about his world. Shimoda was away on a gig and I felt free and open to anything that might happen. He said he was sorry that the film that I had auditioned for never got made. He told me that I reminded him of Julie Christie. How funny, I thought, because of my previous encounter with Julie Christie at a party in New York. I was so flattered by his compliment and when he asked me back to the Carlyle, where he was staying, I said yes. When we arrived at the hotel, he turned to me and said, "I want to be your lover." Even though I was not physically attracted to him, I knew that if I wanted to get to know this fascinating person, I would have to submit. When we walked into his hotel room, he got on the phone and ordered a bottle of wine for us from the hotel bar. We sat beside each other on his bed. He reached over and pulled me close. Then he kissed me softly. Soon, we were lying in bed naked. The lovemaking was warm but not thrilling. I found his stories to be more interesting. He talked of his friend Peter Bogdanovich and how taken Bogdanovich had been with Cybill Shepherd; the sexual energy was so intense that he left his wife. He told me stories about Charles Bluhdorn, the head of Paramount Pictures, how eccentric he was and what it was like to make The Godfather. The first time he spoke with Marlon Brando on the phone, he was shocked that the iconic actor sounded like all the people who imitated him.

On our second date he took me to a café in Little Italy. While we were having cappuccino, two tough-looking guys walked over to our table and said to him, "You directed The Godfather."

"Yes," he replied. Then they said, "Come with us."

For some godforsaken reason we followed them and ended up in the bar next door. It was an old bar with an enormous painting from the 1930s of patrons at the bar. The painting transformed the unfamiliar surroundings and I felt more at ease. While we sat having drinks, they ignored me, but I listened to their conversation about pasta, Italian upbringing, and sordid groups of Mafia characters.

I would see Francis over the next couple of years when he visited New York. He would call to tell me where to meet him. One day as I was sitting at my window, looking down onto West Broadway, I saw him walking up the street with his wife. He looked up and spied me in my window. We both smiled. I watched him turn from his wife and pick up the pay phone on the corner. Suddenly the phone rang in my apartment. I picked it up and he said, "I'm putting this scene in one of my movies."

* * *

I was feeling frustrated with Shimoda. He wasn't contributing anything financially or emotionally. He was lost in New York, alienated from America. I was feeling similarly alienated from him. I complained about his passivity and lack of involvement in creating a life with me. He felt me distancing myself from him and one night he accused me of flirting with a man we had all met together. I told him that the other man seemed alive and interesting. He grew jealous and angry. Suddenly he reached into the kitchen drawer and took out one of the large knives. He came at me with the knife and I thought that he was going to kill me. He chased me several times around the table. Then, breathless, he stopped and we both sat in silence. I knew we were over. I asked him to leave.

I began to work at Food Restaurant. It was a quirky, interesting place filled with unique people. I dated two sculptors at the time, first Joel Shapiro, who did these wonderful, small works of fallen birds, bridges, and houses. He went on to become one of the most famous sculptors of his generation. His work can be seen at the Holocaust Museum in Washington, DC. We would lie in bed and talk in made-up songs, but neither of us was ready for a serious relationship. The other sculptor was Ned Smyth, a very handsome sous chef at the restaurant and a serious artist. He, too, become quite well known and I now live near one of his extraordinary public sculptures. He worked in concrete at the time and as we were exploring the city, we found some new wet concrete being set on Third Avenue. We placed our hands in it.

The oddest characters would show up at Food. I met an actual cowboy, a frame maker who looked as if he'd jumped out of a painting from the Renaissance, and the famous sculptor John Chamberlain, who once chased me down the street, trying to catch me in his arms. The whole atmosphere was a colorfully costumed New York circus.

One day, while I was finishing up my shift at Food, Claude walked into the restaurant. He seemed pleasant and approached me immediately.

"Hi, Sara," he said, "can we go up to your apartment?"

"Of course," I said.

As we left the restaurant, I was filled with a sense of hope. I thought maybe he wanted to reconnect with me. When we entered my apartment, I tried to make him feel welcomed. I immediately offered him a chair and went to get him a glass of water. He idled by the door and said, "No, thank you. I would rather stand."

He looked at me sternly and said, "I can't believe you are working as a waitress and living in this terrible apartment."

"But Claude," I said, "I have a real job and I am supporting myself."

He looked around at the shabby plastered walls and the empty shelves and glared at the old bathtub plopped in the middle of the kitchen.

"Uh!" he gasped. "What are you doing with your life?" I was silent. I did not expect him to throw down such harsh judgments. I couldn't even look at him. I felt the hope for us slowly dying inside me. His bravado seemed to shrink me to the size of a pea. I resisted looking pathetic in the harsh light of his skepticism.

"You know," he finally said, "everyone is so jealous of

me because I don't have to do anything to be famous."
His eyes cooled. "I'm famous just by being the son of
Pablo Picasso."

I couldn't believe that he would brag about such a
thing. Why had he come to visit with me? He was with
some horrible girl at the time and seemed to be in a dark,
confused place. "The court will meet this week and final-
ize the divorce, you don't have to be there. Mr. Wright
will take care of everything.

"Well, I must be going," he said quickly. And with
that, he was out the door, quickly moving down the six
flights, the heavy front door slamming with a thud. I
thought this would be the last time I would see Claude
Picasso. I was wrong.

CHAPTER 21

Having received divorce papers that stated I was no longer married to Claude, I knew that my life was now forever changed. My name was still Sara Lee Ruiz-Picasso and although that no longer seemed right, I wasn't ready to give it up. During the next few years I found myself surrounded by artists living out their dreams. I lived on very little money and at one point went on welfare. I dated a very rich heir to a liquor fortune. He lived in a glamorous apartment above Carnegie Hall and he wanted to be my boyfriend. I wasn't in love with him and though it was tempting to stop struggling for a moment, I could not lie to myself. At this time, around 1972, I went back into therapy at the Karen Horney Clinic with a brilliant analyst named Dr. Melvin Malen. He steered me in a direction that would completely change my life.

I was in group analysis, which is very unusual. I paid five dollars a session, twice a week. There were about eight people in the group. We could express whatever we were feeling and talk about what was happening in our lives. Group was difficult at times because of conflicts that would occur among us. It was hard hearing eight people tell you that you are not being honest with yourself. You didn't have to like everyone in the group but you had to be respectful of them. The feedback I received helped me feel more accepted and accepting. I was confused about who I was supposed to become as opposed to who I really was and what I needed in my life. I stayed in the group for eleven years.

I decided to become serious about my acting, so I enrolled in a class with a very well known acting teacher named Warren Robertson. Robertson's method was to make us stand on the stage, look out at the class of thirty or forty people, and embrace whatever feelings we had at that moment. Robertson was a genius in attacking the repression that stopped us from becoming more alive. He could also see clearly into what we were feeling and say just the right thing to open us up. He made us put it into our work as actors.

"Going off to Japan," he said, "was like being in The Wizard of Oz for you. You have been living in a fairy tale of your own making. I want you to come back to reality so that you can become a fine actress."

Once, during class, I became so upset that I fell down crying.

"Okay, now put that into your monologue," he said.

I had prepared a monologue from Miss Julie by

Strindberg and as I looked out at the class, I could see people crying. I was amazed by the power of taking on a role and performing it with care and honesty.

As I improved as an actor, I began to get more work. I was cast in a play written by David Mamet, Sexual Perversity in Chicago, which had its debut at St. Clement's Church in Manhattan. During the auditions, I noticed a dark, handsome, and very quiet stranger sitting off to the side and I had no idea that it was David Mamet. He cast me as the understudy for the two leads. One night, I went on and a critic from the Village Voice came and called me the next day to tell me that I was better than the original girl. The girl I was standing in for heard about this from someone in the crew in whom I had confided and she had me fired. So much for camaraderie! But the experience made me more intent on becoming a serious actress. I became more committed to studying and went regularly to Warren Robertson's class.

I began to get work on soap operas, commercials, and even some off-Broadway theater. I was cast in One Life to Live as the basketball coach. I don't know what they were thinking since I am only five feet two inches tall, but there I was, the basketball coach to a young Marisa Tomei. Through that experience, I gained more respect for soap opera actors, who have one rehearsal before the scene is filmed. There is a lot of pressure to get it right when filming begins. I guess I was good enough to convince the audience that such a short woman could be a basketball coach.

I joined all the acting unions and was beginning to take pride in what I had accomplished so far. One day, a tall, very handsome man sauntered into my acting class. He had an arresting stare and a quiet intensity. I had seen him perform once before and then briefly met him backstage when he acted in the play Kid Champion alongside my friend Mary Lane Monte. As soon as I saw him onstage I was stricken, like the song "Some Enchanted Evening." Unfortunately he also made me tongue-tied, and I couldn't speak. When I saw him again in class, I was greatly surprised and also happened to be the first one called up to do an exercise that day. I didn't want to act in front of him, but I had to do it. After that, I would sit behind him in class and just stare at him. I was mesmerized by his presence. Finally, I got up enough courage to ask him to do a scene with me. He told me his name was Christopher Walken.

The scene I chose was sexually provocative. (How obvious can one be?) Christopher agreed, but when we were supposed to begin our rehearsals, he was cast in his first film, Roseland. He never returned to class. Six months later, I saw him again. Someone from class was having a party and I brought along a very handsome actor as my date. When I saw Christopher across the room sitting on the arm of a chair, talking to my friend Barbara, the man I was with said to me, "Do you want to talk to him?"

"Yes," I said as I left my date standing there. I walked over and sat down across from Christopher on the opposite arm of the chair. He was talking about therapy and I piped in, "I go to therapy." He stared at me for a long moment, undressing me with his intense eyes, and whispered gently, "Is that right?" His voice was watery and gritty, all at once, like the lapping of a lake. I got a bit sheepish and went over to find my friend Susie. She knew all about my Christopher Walken crush. She had been watching me interact with him and noticed the way he had looked at me. She became very jealous.

"Sara," she said, "you know he's gay, right?" I was devastated because she said it so convincingly. I walked away from her, went to the other end of the room, and looked out the window, feeling devastated that Susie had destroyed a great fantasy of mine in one phrase. I felt a presence next to me and when I looked up Christopher was standing to my left. He looked at me, his blue eyes catching the light from the streetlamps outside the window.

"Are you afraid of me?" he asked. I was completely caught off guard. I swallowed.

"Yes," I replied, stepping backward and failing to notice a standing evergreen plant behind me. As it toppled over, he smiled.

"Let's blow this joint."

We left the party and escaped to some intensely romantic bar where each table had a small lamp with a soft-pink shade. I felt as if I was in a 1940s movie. At one point, I walked into the bathroom to freshen up. Excitement and anxiety were rushing through me all at once. I looked into the mirror, exhaled, and stared at my reflection. Yes, you are really here with him, believe it.

As we sipped our cocktails, I felt pulled into his magnetic stare. He was the most beautiful man I had ever seen. I remained flirty and funny, a mix that he enjoyed. When we finished our drinks, I invited him to my small one-bedroom apartment. When we got there, Christopher looked around with care and appreciation. He embraced me from behind and then turned me around and said he wanted to take me to my bed. My eyes said yes and he picked me up and carried me to the bed. He laid me down on the unmade bed and began to undress me. I shuddered with excitement but I was no longer afraid. I lay there naked as he looked me over. Then he undressed. His body was lean and his erection let me know that he was excited. He began to caress my breasts and then we kissed for a long time. He asked me whether I wanted to fuck and I nodded. He entered me and moved like a dancer. As he went deeper, we kept our eyes fixed on each other.

"I didn't think you would like to fuck," he said.

I smiled. I felt amazingly sexy, desired, and hungry for him. He was happily surprised at how much I enjoyed him.

* * *

I would see Christopher again, off and on for the next two years. The last time we were together, I told him that I had feelings for him. He took a long pause.

"Feelings...they keep changing, they don't mean much," he admitted. "If I don't see you for ten years, it'll always be like it was yesterday."

He was married since the age of twenty and felt marriage didn't have to restrict him. I thought that was exciting and dangerous. He stopped calling after the night that I opened up to him. I guess my feelings did mean something.

I began to feel at sea, bouncing from one love affair to another. I was acting and struggling to survive financially. I had my small Village apartment, but I knew something was missing inside of me. I was thirty-three years old, a time when you have left behind what feels like the invulnerable twenties and you are entering a more serious decade.

When I was dating Joel Shapiro, he'd always tell me to get rid of the name Picasso because it was self-annihilating. Joel was right, and the next chapter in my life would give me the opportunity to leave that name behind.

One night my friend Raphaela Pivetta, a young sculptress, invited me to see the film Le mystère Picasso. Made in the 1950s in Paris, it showed Picasso painting on a scrim in front of the camera. I was curious to see my ex-father-in-law in action and I said that I would meet her at the Film Forum, where it was playing. The lobby of the theater was crowded with people wanting to see this rare film. Just before we were going to buy our tickets, I looked down at the floor in front of me and there was a ten-dollar bill at my feet. It was the exact amount of the ticket. I guess that I wasn't supposed to pay to see him. While watching the film, I felt terrorized by Picasso's intensity and coldness. I was becoming ready to say good-bye to that family name and all that it represented.

At this time, I had recurring dreams about Claude. The theme was always the same: feeling left out. In one of the dreams I was walking around the left bank of Paris and I saw Claude with friends. He told me that he was too busy to talk to me and I should leave. I realized the meaning of these dreams lay in the essential bedrock of my self. In this deep place, I never felt accepted by my family; I felt insignificant and small. After six months of these dreams, I woke determined to seek closure with Claude. I took pen to paper and wrote several letters to him but never received an answer. It seemed he was treating me as if I never existed, just as his father had treated him.

A few months later, I met a man who wrote novels, some of them bestsellers. We got to know each other and he convinced me that I should sue Claude for the paintings that he took from me when we divorced. He introduced me to a lawyer named Peter, a scary and angry German man who decided to take the case. I felt swept along on a wave of defiance. My naïveté about the world helped create the situation. There was a trial; I was followed by detectives and put on a stand by Raoul Felder for six hours. The whole atmosphere made me feel paranoid. One day, at the end of court, I ran into an old friend who had no idea why I was there, and my first thought was that he was set up to follow me. I felt soiled.

Claude and I had one moment alone in the courtroom when I tried to speak to him, and he just looked at me with the same intensity on his face as when he left our apartment the last time with a garbage bag filled with his father's works. In the end, I had one witness and Claude had eleven. The jury voted against me.

I regret having put Claude and myself through this trial. My motivations were several. I felt manipulated at the time of our divorce, as if I had no voice in what I wanted to keep or give up. I was angry that Claude had wiped me out. He treated me like his father had treated him. I needed some closure with Claude and he was not allowing that to happen. I needed to see him and speak with him and unfortunately it happened in a court-room. I regret that it could not have been face-to-face, just between the two of us. Maybe I would get my chance later, under new circumstances.

PART V

A New Factory

CHAPTER 22

I continued to study acting seriously but realized I needed a day job to support myself. I found a job selling advertising for local neighborhood phone directories called blue books. I was able to scrape by with my decent salary but I was getting restless. One day I went to the owner and told him that I wanted to quit.

"Sara, please stay," he pleaded. "I'll give you a raise." I knew that I needed to make more money but I also knew that my feelings of dissatisfaction would not go away.

"Look," he went on, "I'll put you on a new local medical directory." He gestured down the hallway. "Go ask Bill Lavner if you won't make lots more money with this new position." So I went over to Bill Lavner, a colleague with whom I had barely spoken, and asked him what he thought.

"Excuse me, Bill?" I said as I walked into his little office. "I want to quit, but Mr. Gottesman insisted that I talk to you because he says I'll make more money on this new book that you will be working on. Honestly, what do you think?"

"Yes, I think you would," Bill said with confidence.

And with his assurance, I decided to stay. I immediately recognized a gentle strength in Bill and that made it easy for me to stay.

During the next week, I was in closer contact with Bill and he was kind and helpful to me. At the end of the week, all the people in the new book decided to go to a Japanese restaurant for lunch. I was sitting next to Mindy Weinberger, whose voice matched her name. I turned to Mindy near the end of lunch and said to her, "Bill is very nice." She turned to Bill.

"Sara and I both love you." I laughed and Bill looked embarrassed. I then needed to leave the restaurant to make a sales call. Bill asked me, "Well, are you coming back to the office?"

"Yes," I answered as our shared gaze briefly lingered. When I got outside the restaurant I thought, You are in love with Bill Lavner. That is ridiculous!

When I returned to the office later in the day, everyone had decided to go out for drinks and they invited me. Bill sat next to me and I still felt those lunchtime feelings fluttering inside me. Bill walked me home and asked me about my first impression of him.

"You had no presence," I answered honestly.

"I can't believe you just said that."

I laughed and explained that he didn't communicate with me at all. He had made no attempt to speak with me when we were near each other and he had appeared distant. He walked me upstairs and was very curious about how I lived. He was married to someone much younger and lived a very middle-class life in Queens. He had never met a single woman who lived by herself in some quirky apartment in the West Village. He was very gentlemanly and said good night. His gentleness and kindness flowed through him and I was struck by how different he was from any of the men I knew.

Over the next few weeks we would take walks together. Unbeknownst to us the receptionist at work would announce over the loudspeaker that we had left together. Everyone in the office was aware that we were falling in love. On one of our walks on the way to his night class, he told me about his dreams. He wanted to be a comedy writer living in Manhattan. Then he confided to me that he was very unhappy in his marriage. His vulnerability was authentic and I felt our relationship growing into a warm friendship. It seemed as though I had always known him. But he was married and didn't want to sleep with me because he knew it would become very serious for him.

We kept going to lunch and we kept taking walks. I was falling in love with him and realized that the voice I had heard after our first lunch together was prescient. Throughout my life, I've ignored the tiny voices within me. But this time, I listened. On one of our walks Bill told me that he had to buy some new shoes and he was going to go to Florsheim.

"Why would you go there? I know a wonderful Italian men's shoe store." We went to the store I recommended and Bill never looked back. He became the most elegant dresser. Being very visual, I had grown to love fashion as an artistic expression and an illustration of how we feel about ourselves. He just needed someone to give him permission to leave his old world behind and enter a new one.

About a month after we began our relationship, we slept together. He had come over to my apartment and as we kissed on the couch, he took my hand and led me to my bedroom. He gently undressed me and then covered me with kisses. He entered me with care and made love to me. Nothing would be the same between us after that.

I spent Thanksgiving at my brother's house with my mother, father, and my brother's family. My brother's father-in-law was a great German chef and prepared savoy cabbage, sweet potatoes with marshmallows, and a turkey for dinner. My brother's three children sat together, goofing and laughing over jokes. I felt lonelier than I ever had before in my life. I called Bill, who was with his wife and family, and told him that I needed him to be with me. I could no longer be without him.

"I feel the same way," he confessed.

A week after Thanksgiving, Bill moved out of the apartment that he shared with his wife. He rented a studio near Gramercy Park and I helped him pick out furniture. I couldn't believe that what I wanted was actually happening and our relationship was becoming a serious one. Yet I felt a sudden panic. Was I ready to plunge into a romantic committed relationship with another man? I knew my feelings were strong for Bill but I didn't want to be the cause for the end of his marriage. Even though I knew neither of them was happy, I was uncomfortable being the home wrecker.

My feelings began swirling around my past with Claude. I felt tremendous guilt that I was unable to be a good enough wife to Claude and I questioned whether I could make a relationship work with Bill. Because of my lack of connection with my family, I had avoided getting close to a man who was Jewish. With Bill I felt caught, thrown back to my beginnings. I was in turmoil but I knew Bill was important, I just didn't know if I could become a "we." I didn't trust that I had the ability or knowledge to create a lasting relationship and a new family.

Bill wanted me to meet his parents for Passover so he invited me to his family's seder. I had not been to a seder since I was nine years old when I was horrified after taking a swig of Manischewitz wine. I didn't even know what one did at a seder and so I thought to myself, I'll pretend to be Jewish. I asked Bill numerous times whether his parents would accept me since they were upset about his breakup with his wife. He kept reassuring me that all would be okay. The table was set with the seder plate and surrounding the place settings were his brothers, Monte and Michael. His mother was cautious with me but his father was completely open and friendly.

"What was your name before Picasso?" I felt self-conscious to hear the name Picasso being announced in this unsophisticated home; I felt pretentious.

"Schultz," I replied, "Sara Lee Schultz." Then Bill's father smiled, his eyes twinkled.

"You know," he said, "I had a best friend growing up in Brooklyn named Al Schultz."

"Oh?" I said. "I have an uncle named Al Schultz. I should call my father."

Eventually, we figured out that Bill's father and my uncle Al were best friends. That night I also learned that Bill and I had gone to the same Jewish camp, Camp Moodna, but since he was four years younger, we had never met. In that moment I felt my life became one complete circle. I was with my people, my tribe. Suddenly Bill's father jumped up from the table and went into his bedroom. Moments later he emerged with a hand-painted gold, black, and red kimono.

"Do you want this, Sara?" he asked me. "I won it in World War Two when I was stationed in Korea at the time when the Japanese were escaping."

Without hesitation, I looked up and said, "Yes, Mr. Lavner, thank you, I would love to have the kimono."

I was so touched by this warm, welcoming man who

was so real and unaffected. I saw the easy way he included me in their family by giving me something so precious to him. I thought of when I went to meet Claude's family and how his grandmother saw me outside the wall of her home and quickly turned and walked away from me. Yet, as I gazed at my new kimono, everything came into focus—my love of Japan, my Brooklyn-Jewish roots, my new beginning with Bill. The kimono was the most beautiful object in his father's home, yet for years it was hanging in a closet, waiting to be found. In a way, I felt that I had discovered it. I knew I was going to marry Bill.

CHAPTER 23

In one of my acting classes, I met a woman named Barbara Colacello, a seemingly sweet, middle-class girl from Long Island who ran the advertising for Andy Warhol's Interview magazine. After class one day, I told her that I had been working at every kind of job, from being a waitress at jazz clubs to selling local ads in neighborhood yellow pages. I was done with day jobs. I felt ready to reenter the art world that Claude had introduced to me. I missed the excitement of something more mysterious, glamorous, and challenging.

"Oh, you know, you would be great working for Andy at Interview."

"Well, I knew Andy from when I was married to Claude," I explained. "We would visit the Factory."

"Perfect. I will arrange for you to meet him and his associate, Fred Hughes, and my brother Bob, who are now running the Factory."

I was giddy. I adored Andy and his work. I was trans-fixed with his colorful entourage of characters—the dark-haired, sultry beauty Ultra Violet; the wildly outgo-ing, curly-haired Viva; and the cool blonde, Nico, from Sweden. I thought this opportunity would be a good change in my life. After my separation from Claude, and the rejection by some of our friends, I wanted to reenter and be accepted on my own terms.

I went to speak with Fred Hughes, Andy's right-hand man, who I had met when I was married to Claude. He jumped at the chance to have a Picasso working with Andy and I was instantly hired to help Barbara run the advertising department for Interview. I wasn't yet ready to give up the name Picasso or the entitlements that went along with it. I had got used to having that power in the world. It didn't make me feel more whole as a person but it was a quick fix; the name had a secret magic that would beguile the people around me.

The Factory at Union Square was open and airy, with ceilings that rose high above our heads. There were mas-sive wood and glass doors that opened to a labyrinth of rooms. The space felt more old-style European than modern New York, an odd contrast to the nature of what went on in those rooms. Andy painted and held lun-cheons in the Factory and always played host to a lively mix of artists, celebrities, groupies, art dealers, and peo-ple who advertised in the magazine. Although he seemed elusive and cloudlike, he was sharply observant of all that went on around him. Most days he quietly moved around the Factory, painting on the floor in a small corner of this enormous loft. He appeared lithe and thin, a ghost suddenly appearing out of nowhere behind me one moment, only to quickly disappear again. I always wondered what he concealed under his coiffed white wig. With all his eccentricities, I found him to be very kind. He was one of the few famous artists who freely and generously gave away his work to his friends and employees. I never heard a harsh word out of his mouth. Actually, I think he had Fred or Bob take care of the unpleasant situations.

There was an expansive maple wood table in one room where Andy would host his luncheons. I often witnessed the wild theater that went on around that table. I remember Geoffrey Beene discussing the color red with Andy and a small gathering of socialites.

"Women either hate it or love it," he declared. "But it's a strong, sexy color and so I use it." There was a wealthy Upper East Side lady who was part of his entourage that day. I watched as she listened to Geoffrey's every word with rapt attention and then told us how she would get a massage every day. I tried to imagine how wonderful that might be.

I will never forget the luncheon when we hosted an important woman from Christie's auction house. She appeared statuesque in her Armani suit and her ginger hair coiffed like a dense brioche. Her stilettoed feet never seemed to touch our plebian ground as she hovered around the office. During the meeting, Andy had his tape recorder on and moved about the room, surreptitiously snapping photos on his camera. I engaged this Englishwoman by asking her what she liked about New York and encouraged her to speak of her home in England. She began to relax and loosen up a bit. When she left, I breathed a sigh of relief.

"Andy was very impressed with how you handled her," Fred confided. "She was not easy." I took that comment as a great compliment from a team of people I very much wanted to impress and who were so good at using the world to their advantage.

There were all kinds of odd people working for Andy. There was this nouveau riche girl named Gail who was the most pretentious person I had ever met, and that's including the over-the-top people I met while married to Claude. She was always talking about her Lilly Pulitzer clothes and her new house that her very WASPy husband had just bought for them as a weekend retreat. One day, after she heard that I was engaged, she stopped me in the hallway.

"I heard that your fiancé was married before. Did his former wife get all the family jewels?"

"I don't think there were any family jewels," I said blankly. She retreated in horror as I took a deep breath. This encounter made it blatantly clear that my values were quite different from these people's. I loved beautiful objects, jewels, furniture, paintings, but they did not define me. They reflected parts of me, and I admired these materials, not idolized them.

Another woman named Carol was the drudge of the office and worked very hard but was caught up in knowing everyone's pedigree. She noticed my Cartier three gold band ring that Claude had given to me. "Oh, Sara, I love your ring." I hadn't thought about it, but the ring began to look odd on my finger. I felt I had to say goodbye in order to someday put another ring on that finger. "Do you want to buy it?" I asked her. She was immediately interested. "I'll sell it to you for fifty dollars."

"I'll bring in the cash tomorrow."

I felt that I was betraying Claude once again by selling this beautiful ring. A part of me wanted to keep it and yet I knew that I had to move on and let it go. The next day she brought in her fifty dollars. I took the ring off my finger and handed it over to her.

* * *

Andy loved photographing and recording everyone around him. I think this activity kept him at a safe distance from people. He was fascinated by all the commercial aspects of the world and instinctively knew how to mine them. He was perplexed about why I wouldn't exploit the name Picasso. "Can't you make money with it somehow?" he said, looking at me in utter confusion. I felt uncomfortable, but not insulted, when he posed that question to me. I knew that part of the reason I was working for him was that I had that name. But I also knew that this was Andy's approach to the world. Actually, I found it amusing and also sad. In a way, I felt as if I were talking to a very successful child.

I was also involved with a new relationship and didn't want to harm my connection to Bill. Now, years later, with much more maturity, I don't have to deny my tie to all parts of my past, including being part of that family and revealing what happened to me and how it formed the person I am today.

One day a new intern stepped through the doors of the Factory. She had blond, shoulder-length hair, striking sky-blue eyes, and was lushly curvy—I thought she could easily be wearing a dirndl. "This is Pingel," Andy announced. "She is the Princess Ingeborg Schleswig-Holstein and she will be working here with us."

At last, we had a real princess at The Factory. She was very charming and we liked each other immediately. I was curious to see what a real one was like. She and another intern named Peter Estersohn and I would hang out together. She wanted to be a painter and Peter wanted to become a photographer. One day, she and Peter came over to my tiny apartment in the West Village. "Oh, I've got to go shopping!" Pingle exclaimed. "I'm going home for the holidays and I've got to buy some ball gowns." She said this matter-of-factly, with no pretensions. Pingle had a sparkle about her that made her easy to like. I had never heard such a sentence uttered before and I tried to imagine the feeling of attending lavish royal balls in castles. She was not awkward at all and seemed so comfortable as a "princess." My mother had served me, never sitting down to eat with me, never allowing me to do any housework. This led me to becoming Mrs. Sara Picasso. Yet, I had no foundation to back me up and here was the "real deal," whose sense of entitlement wasn't something I could respect. I felt myself wanting to become part of the world that most people lived in.

Andy seemed to like me. He could relax around me and he sensed my honesty and enthusiasm. We developed a trusting relationship and I began to sell his art. I tried to get a very rich woman I had met to purchase a portrait that he would paint of her. "Don't forget," he instructed, "one for twenty-five thousand but only charge forty thousand for two."

I often felt this new art world I had entered was superficial. But I loved being surrounded by the art that Andy was working on, on the floor in a corner of this large loft. He engendered an environment of freedom and creativity. Yet, the social side of the operation was another matter. One day when I was coming to work, Claude's sister Paloma entered the elevator with me. I hadn't seen her in many years. She said hello and I greeted her warmly. She said that Fred had told her that I was working at the Factory. When we got to the Factory floor, she exited the elevator without a good-bye and I felt she had erased me in a mere instant. That was how Claude and Paloma were trained to deal with people. They had both been dismissed from their father's life for no reason, except for the jealousy of their stepmother, Jacqueline.

In their family, erasure was a legacy passed down from father to children.

Bob Colacello would often be on the phone with socialites like Monique Vooren or Ultra Violet and I would hear him saying in a defensive voice, "We can't invite you. It's a very select group."

Fred Hughes, who was by Andy's side for many years, was the main connector to all the socialites and kept telling me how he almost married Paloma. I knew Fred was gay so I became a bit perplexed. Then again, most of what unfolded at the Factory perplexed me. I decided not to question Fred; he seemed to need this fantasy.

After a year, I was offered a job at Art in America, mainly because of my name, and they even doubled my salary, so I had to accept. When I told Andy that I would be leaving, he looked up over his glasses and smiled. "Just make sure you become famous." Before I left, I popped my head into Fred's office. I remembered that I was owed some of my salary. "Fred? Remember the three hundred dollars you owe me?"

"Oh! Of course, darling! I forgot about that."

"It's okay, I don't think I want the money. I was thinking, maybe, one of Andy's pieces?" He thought for a moment.

"Well, no one wants the silk screen of the electric chair. I'll give you one of those."

I have always been proud of this acquisition, especially after giving up other valuable art from my first marriage. It is now worth a great deal more than three hundred dollars.

* * *

In later years when I would run into Andy, he was always friendly. "Are you acting?" he would ask. "Are you famous yet?"

"No, not yet, Andy," I would say, amused.

I would think about Claude and all his warnings about the trappings of fame, which he himself fell victim to after we parted. I was becoming less interested in fame for fame's sake and more interested in finding out what I really cared about in life. The voices that I had ignored in the past, those deep whispers, were getting louder.

Taking the job at Art in America was a big mistake. They gave me the worst territory and thought because my name was Picasso, people would hand over ad money to me with little resistance. My boss, Susan B. Anthony— yes, that was her real name—was the opposite of the real Susan B. Anthony; values or people mattered very little to her. They sent me to Scottsdale, Arizona, to sell advertising space to area art galleries, but I didn't know how to drive a car. I met with a very wealthy man who dabbled as a painter and he became my chauffeur. Bill came to spend a few days with me and this man actually gave us his home while he and his wife went to stay with relatives. Bill and I were amazed that we could go outside and pick an orange or a grapefruit right off the tree.

After about six months, Susan B. Anthony had me fired. I will always be grateful because it threw me right back into acting full-time. I began to work seriously as an actress in commercials, film, and theater. I began a business with an actor named Dick Rizzo where casting agents would meet actors in my small two-bedroom apartment. I was trying to be entrepreneurial with my career, but the most important opportunity that came out of being fired was that I had time to concentrate on getting married.

I wanted to marry Bill but he was hesitant because his divorce was so fresh. So we stopped talking about getting married. A few months passed and then one night, my hair wet from a shower and dressed in my flannel pajamas, I was approached by Bill. "There was something I wanted to ask you before you went into the shower and now I forgot."

"Well, try to remember what you were doing before I went into the shower and it will come back to you."

"Oh, now I remember," he said. "Will you marry me?"

I was speechless. Did I feel assured enough to know what I really wanted? Bill was getting nervous.

"Well...answer!" he insisted, letting out a nervous laugh. I looked at him and really took him in. I realized how much he had come to resonate in my life: his integrity, his honesty, and his kindness. He accepted who I was, the girl from Brooklyn, the wild adventurer, the confused fame seeker, and the caring woman. Then I thought about his ability to always make me laugh out loud. There was one time he came home from a business trip and took a picture of a woman out of his briefcase and put it under his pillow. I asked him who she was and he said, "It doesn't mean anything."

"No?" I said. "Who is she?"

"It really doesn't mean anything," he replied, and then he told me it was just someone who was looking for a job and wanted him to give her picture and résumé to his boss. I cherished his sense of humor.

"Yes," I finally replied to Bill. "Yes."

Before I married Bill, I realized that I wanted to have his name. How would I let the world know that I was finally giving up the name Picasso? One day, I was walking through Tiffany's and dreaming of the special jewelry that I wanted, when I passed the birth announcement display case. There was a printed card with a smaller card placed on top, a small pink bow attaching it to the larger card. I was taken by its perfect elegance. A flash of inspiration struck me and I realized that this would be the way to announce to the world that I had changed my name. I was no longer Sara Picasso.

We got married that May in the rabbi's study at the largest temple in Manhattan, Temple Emanu-El, followed by a luncheon at Central Park's Tavern on the Green. The night before we got married we went out to eat, but the restaurant wouldn't take credit cards.

"That is so stupid not to take credit cards, what a ridiculous restaurant," Bill yelled as we crossed the street.

"They have every right to do the business the way they want to. You're just overreacting." He scowled at me.

"You are so wrong and I'm never going there again."

"Yes, you will," I said, and then we arrived at John's Pizzeria. He looked at me.

"I don't even want to have dinner with you." I stepped off the sidewalk, pulling myself away from him.

"Well, I hope you die," I shouted.

Immediately we both cracked up laughing and threw our arms around each other. Our sense of humor has helped us through many tough times together. I always advise people not to see their betrothed on the night before their wedding. I think there is actually an old Jewish tradition in which the bride and groom don't see each other for a week before the wedding and then the groom gets to lift the veil of his bride before the ceremony just to make sure he is marrying the right person. Bill's sense of humor also surfaced the week before the wedding when he was picking me up at my group therapy appointment. My therapist, Dr. Melvin Malen, left the room before the rest of the group. When I came out Bill told me that Dr. Malen had handed him a note that read, "Don't do it." Bill was always the prankster. His sense of humor and perspective on life was so fresh in contrast to Claude's maudlin mood. He did not come from a well-educated and harmonious family, but it was a caring family. There was a lot less glitter than the Picassos had. Bill's family was average and unglamorous, but they had love. I had shunned these types of people in the past, threatened that they would diminish my specialness. But now I understood their value and how healing it felt to be part of them.

The morning of our wedding was filled with omens. I awoke to the sound of Japanese wind chimes trilling over the soft hum of New York traffic. In all the years I lived in my tiny one-bedroom apartment, I had never heard this sound before. Once when I was living in Japan, I was walking down the street and feeling quite homesick. I looked up to a balcony strung with clothes drying in the wind and heard the wind chimes hanging near the window. The sound filled me with peace. In that moment of feeling so far away from the familiar, those chimes soothed my anxious heart. Now, on the morning of my second marriage, I listened to the bright, tinny music and thought it to be a good omen, a sound connecting my past with my future with Bill.

I wore a white organdy dress with lavender trim that I had specially designed for me. I loved that I helped create the design and it felt like me. I thought about the dress I wore for my wedding to Claude, the one my mother had crocheted for me. I wore it to please her and she had seemed happy, but I was not truly comfortable wearing it. My mind drifted to that day when I felt like I needed to keep my marriage to Claude a secret from the public. But with Bill, I could proudly and publicly declare my love for him.

Meanwhile, Bill took the limousine uptown to be with a friend. As he stopped at a light in front of the Waldorf Astoria, Johnny Carson passed in front of the car. Johnny Carson was one of Bill's idols. Humor is so important to Bill and we both had good omens that day.

CHAPTER 24

When Claude and I were together, we would imagine our life in the future. Claude talked about having some power over his father's works and placing sculptures in public places for all people to enjoy. He never talked about wanting to be a father, I think, because he never had an image in his mind of what a decent father was. I had unconscious desires to create a family, but they were buried within a maze of hurt stemming from a deep sadness and disappointment with my own family. The wounds were so sharp and cavernous after Claude suffered his father's rejection; I think he was not able to feel open to the idea of being a father himself at that time. I knew Claude had nurturing instincts, but they came out in odd ways. Instead of having children, we adopted three cats and he bought a blender that could also cook hot things.

Bill was different. I was comfortable with him from our first walk together. I trusted him and knew he could be a family man, one who would read to his children and hold them close to his heart.

In 1983, two years after getting married, Bill and I were seriously thinking about becoming parents. But instead of becoming a real mother, I was cast as Momma Womble on a potential television series that had been a big hit in England. I played a giant hamsterlike mother creature. In my desire to become a real mother, I became a Womble Mother; not exactly the role I envisioned for my life at that moment. I suppose one has to be very specific when one wishes for something. Nothing happened with Momma Womble—it was never picked up for American TV. However, I became quite determined to become a human mother.

For months, Bill and I were "trying" but nothing was happening. Our doctor administered many tests to find out why. Finally, he injected dye into my fallopian tubes and the next month I was pregnant. We were so happy and then a few days later, I began to have intense pain and bleeding. I fainted in Bill's arms and the next morning when we went to the doctor, he tried to find the baby using a sonogram. He looked at me and said, "You are having an ectopic pregnancy. You must go immediately to the hospital for an emergency operation."

Tears fell down my face as Bill and I hurried out of the office to find a taxi to take us to the emergency room. The nurses rushed me into surgery and within twenty minutes, the doctors were operating on my ruptured fallopian tube. They removed the tube and the embryo that was stuck inside of it. Three months later, adhesions formed and wrapped themselves around my intestines and choked all the gas inside. Again, I went to the emergency room and after six hours of intense pain, they decided to operate to save my life once again. On the way into the operating room, our family doctor, Dr. Robilotti, looked at Bill with a reassuring smile. "Don't worry," he said. "I have a nice Italian girl for you."

I knew it was funny, but I had completely lost my sense of humor. They opened me up, cut the adhesions, and after five days of only eating Jell-O, I was back home.

Bill and I did not give up. We kept trying to get pregnant. Finally the doctor did another operation and realized that the other tube was also blocked. The doctor met Bill in my room while I was still in the OR and told him that I would not be able to have children. Bill stood at the window, looking at the trees below.

"Maybe we shouldn't tell Sara right away," the doctor said.

"No, you don't know Sara," remarked Bill. "I will tell her immediately."

When I was taken back to the room, Bill sat on the crisp white sheets of the bed and told me. I felt a deep pain run down the center of my body and I fell silent.

When Bill and I got home, I was resting in my bed and Bill was holding my hand. It felt like someone suddenly punched me and I began to heave and sob. It was the deepest cry that I have ever experienced.

My only option was to undergo invitro fertilization. At that time I was covered under the Screen Actors Guild's health care plan and tried to convince them to absorb the cost of the procedure. Bill thought otherwise.

"You have suffered enough," he said. "I don't want you to go through any more pain." His voice felt warm, and when I looked in his eyes, I believed him.

"What does it mean to have a child?" he asked. "It means to love a child, that is what is important." At that moment I thought he was the kindest and wisest man I had ever known. We decided to adopt.

We chose to adopt from Korea and found an adoption agency in Long Island called New Beginnings. We were interviewed and filled out long applications, explaining why we should be selected as parents. It took a total of six months for our daughter Lilly YeJin Rachel Lavner to come to America. Mrs. Park, our counselor at the agency, received Lilly's picture at six weeks old and decided that she was meant for us. She arrived on Labor Day (I thought that was appropriate) in September 1985 at JFK Airport. She was three months old, chubby, beautiful, and hungry. Servicemen and Korean citizens carried the children off the plane for all the waiting families. We were in a corner of the airport, waiting by the elevators for them to come through customs. We had bottles of milk and some diapers. Just a week before, I was visiting my neighbor and her baby and I rehearsed putting a diaper on a baby; I put it on backward. I was hoping that some instinct would kick in when Lilly arrived. The elevator doors opened and out came five Korean babies. We were told to stand. With my heart pounding, I waited to hear whose name would be called first. They called our name and my daughter was handed to me.

"Hello, I'm your mother." Lilly looked up at me and smiled. When we sat down, she immediately began to cry. "Bill," I said in a panic, "you have to get the bottle together, I think she's hungry!" He didn't know what to do. "Ask that woman over there," I said, wildly pointing. "She looks like a grandmother."

The older woman came over to us and prepared the bottle. I sat holding the bottle to Lilly's mouth as she drank all the milk. We stood up and then boarded the bus for Manhattan. There were only two seats left.

The next few days were like being cuddled in a soft cashmere blanket. We were so happy to get to know her. Everything was focused on Lilly. All the grandparents came and then our friends came and fed her, changed her, and played music and sang to her. A week after her arrival, she broke out in spots and had a high fever. The doctor told me to take her to the hospital. He told us that her white blood count was going down, so I slept by her bed every night. I have never before or since felt suicidal, but I did on the third day. If she were to be taken from me then, I didn't know if I would want to go on.

They called an infectious diseases expert to the hospital because they wanted to perform a spinal tap. She was a young doctor and I checked her out from head to toe before letting her see my child.

"How old are you?" I asked, rather aggressively. The nurse turned to me.

"Maybe you should take a Valium, Mrs. Lavner."

"No, thank you," I said. "I don't take drugs." The doctor looked Lilly over.

"It's just a common virus," she concluded.

We took her home and she soon began to recover. Lilly had a tiny room, but it was so charming. A handmade black-and-white polka-dot standing bookshelf with a large Asian doll and a small handmade pink and blue rattle doll stood in one corner. A Tiffany rabbit bank; a blue, white, and pink bunny blanket; a crib; and a changing table all neatly fit together with one sunny window. She was beautiful and her smile sparkled.

Lilly began speaking at nine months old and has never stopped. I was in a taxi with her when she looked up from my arms and uttered her first words.

"Juice," she said. My face brightened.

"That can't be your first word," I said, "it's so unromantic!"

Her practicality in life was there from the very beginning. (After all, her second word was Cheerios!) At three years old she wrote a commercial about gum, and at six she paid her classmate one dollar to do the drawings in her school project. When I inquired as to why she had done this, Lilly said that the girl was a better artist (and truth be told, she was). Quite strong-willed, she also liked to take over situations and excelled at whatever she tried. To this day we are so happy to have her as our daughter.

Lilly was aware of her adoption, and the fact that she did not look like us, from the very beginning. I told her that some children are born in their mother's bellies and some are born in their mother's hearts. When she was three years old, she looked up at me and said, "I was in another woman's belly crying out for you, my mommy."

CHAPTER 25

We would visit my parents in Flushing, Queens, and eat at the many Korean restaurants throughout the neighborhood. Sitting down for dinner, my mother laughed when she saw the little dried fish and the marinated bean sprouts. "What are those things, how do they taste?" I assured her: "Just try it, I think you will like it. It's something new." She dug her fork in to gather up the small spears of fish and cautiously slipped them into her mouth. "They're good"—she beamed—"what else should I try?!" I quickly ordered a tofu dish and a meat dish and told the waitress not to make it spicy. She gobbled them up and I could see how well she was responding to this new adventure in something so unknown to her. I wanted to reach across the table and hug her, but we didn't do that and so my voice embraced her as if we were finally meeting in the middle of a bridge.

Slowly, as my mother and father reached the ages of eighty-six and eighty-nine, respectively, they stopped cleaning their apartment, they didn't take the same care of their clothing, and they refused to have a cleaning lady whom I arranged to pay for. My mother actually went by herself to Atlantic City and let a stranger walk her home from the bus. When my father fell in the street and refused to stay in the hospital in Queens because he wanted to come to Manhattan, I found him a room within hours. A few months later he was in the hospital again and I brought my mother to live with us for a few days. At one point, I took her to a drugstore to get her medication and then left it with her in the car because I had forgotten something in the store. When I returned, I told her that we would go back to her house, before we went to visit my father in the hospital, and I would crush her pills so she could swallow them. My father would always complain about how he had to crush the pills for her. She turned to me and said, "Oh, I took them already." I stared blankly at her and said, "How could you swallow them without them being crushed and having no water?" She said innocently, " Oh, I just swallowed them." Had she pretended to be a helpless child all these sixty-five years with my father?

So when things became overwhelming, my brother Hy swooped in like a white knight to "save them" and took them to live in a nursing home in Pittsburgh. He accused me of not helping them and in doing so wiped out all my years of caring for them when he never came to visit them. He ordered me to buy my mother new underwear and I was unable to stand up to him and his accusatory voice. His need to make me a bad person seemed to blind him to who I really was. I've never understood why he was so filled with judgment and hatred.

At the nursing home in Pittsburgh, my father ended up being violent with one of the nurses. First he hit my mother and then he tried to punch the nurse when she served him his dinner. He was sent to a psychiatric hospital for six weeks and when he returned to the nursing home, my mother and father were separated and lived on different floors. My brother did not put a phone in my mother's room and so I had no other contact with her. I asked her social worker to arrange a time for me to speak with my mother in her office.

"Hi, Mom," I said in a quiet voice, "how are you feeling?"

"I'm good, I play bingo with the women. How is Bill and the children?"

"They're all good," I responded, feeling her presence fade.

"Yes, Bill is quiet and Lilly and David are so nice." We spoke for another few moments and said good-bye, and it was our final good-bye. I felt she was free after sixty-five years of many restrictions from my father and she sounded peaceful.

Two days later, in the early morning, my mother walked into the bathroom, fell to the tiled foor, and died. My brother called to tell me. I was relieved that she and I had finally spoken. I felt good that she died quickly, with no lingering suffering. She entered this world being passed around at a wedding and she left instantly with little fanfare but easily.

Her funeral was two days later and I flew to Pittsburgh with the children and Bill. I called my brother and said, "Can you pick us up at the airport? We don't know how to get to the funeral home."

"No, I'm busy," he said.

"Okay, then give me the address." He read me the name and address of the funeral home and hung up the phone. An hour later he called back, "The limo won't charge extra, so I'll have them pick you up at the airport."

"Thank you," I said simply. I couldn't believe that he held on to his anger at this moment in our family's history, this final moment of sharing our parents. I wasn't even angry, just amazed at his awfulness.

We walked into the funeral home and I noticed how empty it felt. My eyes went to the dark purple brocade on the curtains that seemed to cover everything. Then I saw my mother's casket, her body in the wood box. I told Bill to take the children outside to play and I would find my brother. As I walked into a side room I saw Hy seated with people I didn't know. I noticed a piece of black lace on a tray. I put it on my head with a bobby pin and I sat down in a chair next to my brother. As I sat there, the silence in the room grew. My eye began to twitch. I looked over at my brother; he looked bloated, his eyes tired. I remembered how blond, blue-eyed, and handsome he was as a boy. Finally I said, "Who are these people?" Seeminly startled by my directness, he turned to me and mumbled an apology and then introduced them to me. I knew none of them but nodded to each one in turn.

When the funeral ended, we all went to the cemetery to bury my mother. Lilly made a drawing of a flower and threw it down into the grave as the casket was being lowered into the ground. Then we all went into the limousine to take my brother and sister-in-law back to their house for shiva. Even though we were going back to the airport, we had some time to spend with my family at shiva. But we were never invited inside the house. When the car stopped at their home, my brother and sister-in-law began to argue about getting us some sandwiches to take on the plane. I felt as if I were floating above them and watched as though I were observing two strange animals. My brother went into his house and my sister-in-law said to me, "I guess the next time we see you will be Lilly's wedding." I stared at her and said nothing, but I thought to myself, no, you will never be invited. Then my brother emerged, carrying a small bag of sandwiches. "Here you go," he said, waving the bag toward me, "for the road." I didn't see him again for seventeen years.

Meanwhile, back at the nursing home, my father's health was swiftly failing. For weeks he was bedridden, relying on his nurses to help him every day. The morning after my mother died, a young doctor went to my father's room to tell him his wife had died. My father, who appeared to be sleeping, was struggling to breathe.

Very quickly the doctor discovered that my father was slipping into a coma. At the end of the next week, my father died, never regaining consciousness. My father never knew that my mother had died and he never knew of her death, I thought that was a blessing.

I always feel odd when people tell me how grief-stricken they feel when their parents die. For me, I felt empty of feeling. Is there something wrong with me, am I a bad person for not weeping as I buried my parents? My brother Victor died seven years before my parents and my brother Hy died nineteen years after them. And I never cried for any of them. I did not know what greiving felt like but I wanted to know. I would tell people that they were lucky to feel sad. I struggled to feel connected to them in life and now in their deaths, I felt nothing.

CHAPTER 26

As Lilly got older, she would often ask about her birth mother, wondering what she looked like and worrying whether she had enough to eat. I always encouraged her to share her feelings about her adoption; it was her right. When she asked me what her birth mother looked like, I would tell her to look in the mirror. I promised her that someday we would try to find this woman.

When Lilly was two, I felt a strong urge to give her a sibling. The people across the hall, Betty and Nathalie, were willing to move downstairs so that we could break through the walls and enlarge our living space for another child. Miss Alberti, our eccentric and very old spinster Italian landlady, liked us and granted us permission. She looked like your average bag lady, but owned half the Village.

Our son, David, also from Korea, arrived on December 22, 1988, at nineteen months old. He had been traumatized by being given up at one year old by his birth mother and then he contracted a severe case of chicken pox. He was taken to a hospital and left there for three weeks, alone and frightened. He was then given to a foster mother, and after five months he was taken out of her arms and flown to America.

When Lilly, Bill, and I greeted David at the airport, I was so excited. I immediately took him into my arms. He looked at me and began to cry hysterically. Bill took him from me and he calmed down. We received a letter the next day from the adoption agency that offered some advice. Because he had been in the foster care system during his early formative years, David would choose one person onto whom he would project all of his fear and anger. The person he chose to rebel against, unfortunately, was me. Any stranger could come into the house and hold him and he would be fine, everyone but his new mother. Bill was becoming exhausted by how demanding this situation was on him and Lilly was visibly upset. She would hold him on her little lap and they would watch TV together but she found it all confusing. By the third day, my friend Marci came by and said, "You must have everyone leave the house and you must force him to let you hold him." I believed that she was right.

Everyone left and he began to scream hysterically. I grabbed him as he was trying to pull away and took him into his bedroom. I sat down in the middle of the floor on the gray industrial carpeting and didn't let go for what seemed like forever. Gradually his breathing slowed down and he relaxed into my body. I whispered to him,

"It's okay, I'm your mother now and I will never leave you."

Because of his emotional problems, stemming from his early abandonment, it would take another six months before I felt we had fully bonded. One warm summer day, he and I sat in the grass, looking out onto a lake and at the same moment, we turned to each other, our eyes smiling. We quietly acknowledged that trust was beginning to blossom.

We settled into a steady, stable family life. I wanted to create family rituals, family dinners, and a sense of closeness that I had never experienced because my brothers were so much older than I. David was talented and unusual from the start. At three years old, his drawings were different from the other children's drawings. He did a painting that was all blue with a thin red line just at the very top; it was like an early abstract expressionist painting by Adolph Gottlieb. One of the fathers at the nursery school was an artist and he went out of his way to talk to me about David's unusual artistic talents. At eight, our son did a triptych drawing of a green and yellow spotted dragon with black spiked hair and black and white extended arms, flanked on each side by a panel of day and a panel of night. The day has a yellow sun, clouds, and winged birds. The night has a yellow moon and stars with a black background. The dragon's head and one arm spill into the day. His drawing so impressed the vice principal of his school that she hung it in her office for the entire year. David had a preternatural understanding of proportion in his drawings and a keen sense of color and balance.

When David was four and Lilly was six, we decided to visit a lovely Japanese woman whom I had met in Washington Square Park. She was from a small town, and since we had shown her around New York City, she invited us to stay with her and her family in her town of Shimada, Japan. All our friends thought we were crazy to travel so far with two small children. But we firmly believed it was important for David and Lilly to experience the Far East, the place of their origin.

On the morning of our departure, Bill and I managed to get Lilly and David up at five o'clock and out of bed by giving them a chocolate candy bar. I knew the sugar alone would keep them awake until we reached the airport and boarded the plane. They were amazing little troupers. When we arrived in Japan, my friend Gogi, a Japanese film director, met us at the airport and took us to his apartment, our new home for the duration of the trip. Because of the time difference, we all took a nap and awoke a few hours later groggy and cranky. I found David intently watching a Japanese program on the television. He turned to me and said, "I look like them!"

Eventually we traveled to Shimada and stayed in our friend's home with her mother, father, and hundred-year-old grandmother. We ventured to the town pool. Both our children jumped in and suddenly we realized we couldn't find them. It was the first time that Lilly and David had ever been surrounded by other Asian children.

We were jolted into this new reality. Yet, everyone was incredibly welcoming. About six girls came back to the house and all the children decided to take a bath in the wooden Japanese tub. David found himself surrounded by naked girls, something he didn't seem to mind at all. We all giggled, children and parents alike.

One night, my friend Kayoko dressed Lilly and me in flowered kimonos and David and Bill in blue and white yukatas. We walked a few blocks and visited one of her neighbors. It was a large house and the grandmother greeted us at the door. I immediately spotted a very elaborate paper Japanese doll enclosed in a clear plexiglass stand. It was explained to me that it was the grandmother's creation. We went upstairs to have tea with the husband and wife; we sat on the tatami floor as the husband went into his closet and took out print after print of famous Japanese classic prints from the 1800s. I asked whether these were original works and he proudly answered yes. As we walked home, I asked Kayoko why they were not displayed or in a museum and she told me, "I didn't have any idea that he owned these valuable works of art. In Japan, people often keep art in their closets and no one ever knows." I was definitely living in a different world; everything was the opposite of what I expected. The next day, the doll was delivered to Kayoko's home as a present for me. In Japan, it is dangerous to say you like something because then they must give it to you. I had forgotten this tradition. I thought, well, what about the original Japanese prints?

Back in New York, I decided to go back to school for a master's degree in drama therapy. We lived down the block from New York University and I could run to class in five minutes. I wanted to ensure the steady employment and financial security I needed to help raise my children. Bill completely supported my decision and his mother often babysat the children. I loved being a mother and a wife but I knew that there was something missing from my life.

Within the first year of studying for my degree, I began to discover exactly what was missing. I realized I needed to challenge myself intellectually by diving into my studies in a way I had never done before. I became a straight-A student for the first time in my life and started listening to and learning from a new place within me. I realized just how powerfully damaging my brother Hy's attitude toward me had been. In one of the psychology classes that I took, Theories of Personality, I received one of the highest marks in the class. In drama therapy terms, it would be explained that this was a new role that I had never been cast in before and I didn't know my lines. I went up to the teacher and asked him to add up my essay marks again because he must have made a mistake. He looked at me like I was some alien from the planet of Low Esteem and said, "No, Sara, this is your mark." It took me some time to warm to my new role as an academic achiever.

After graduation, I worked for five years at Gracie Square Hospital as a drama therapist. I was humbled by the difficulties of the mentally ill and how much these patients struggled to function every day. I tried to balance being a mother, wife, and therapist. I felt stretched in multiple directions, but a growing desire to be all that I could be was taking over. I realized I didn't need to be Mrs. Picasso to be worthwhile; I was finding the worthwhile Sara. I was elegantly juggling much more than my family ever thought that I could. Little did I know that during this great height of personal achievement, a new test for me was right around the corner, bringing circumstances that would forever alter my life.

CHAPTER 27

Of our two children, Lilly was the most concerned about finding her birth parents. She would sometimes cry because she was afraid that her birth mother was starving. I knew I wanted to find her and David's birth parents because it was an important part of their identity and they had a right to that knowledge. When Lilly was eleven, we contacted the orphanage in Korea and inquired about searching for Lilly's birth mother. The agency quickly responded, reporting that they found her on a remote, volcanic island called Ulleungdo in the middle of the ocean. The postman was able to find her so quickly because she happened to work for the richest woman on the island in the only gas station on the island. She also had a name that was one of a kind: Noh-Bu Dol. Lilly's birth mother wrote a letter to us stating that she could now die with no regret, knowing that Lilly was safe. Bill and I waited to find the right moment to tell Lilly. One night she was lying on our bed and asked a question about Korea. We looked at each other and knew that the moment had arrived.

"Lilly," I said, "we found your birth mother and she has sent you a letter." Her face lit up like the sun. After I read the letter to Lilly, she glowed and asked whether she could sleep in my bed. Bill slept on the couch that night. As Lilly fell asleep next to me, I felt so reassured that she was my daughter and that our love would endure whatever was to come next.

We wanted to go to Korea as soon as possible and decided to go on an organized tour. We found a Korean Homeland Tour that was specifically for Korean adoptees and their families. When we arrived in Seoul, our tour bus took us around the city, passing the old standing gate that had been the entrance to the city a thousand years before. There was a river running through the middle of the city and ancient gardens amidst tranquil ponds against modern skyscrapers and the hustle and bustle of city life. We felt in touch with the ancient and the new all at the same time.

When we stopped for lunch, everyone exited the bus ahead of me, so I remained in my seat. I looked out the window and saw Lilly with the other children waiting by the side of the bus. It was the first time I had ever seen Lilly surrounded by a backdrop of Korean people, her native tribe. When she looked up at me, I saw my own expression on her face for a few moments. The feeling was mystical, and then I realized that I needed that new canvas to see how she was so like me on the inside.

Before we left for Korea, we wrote to Lilly's birth mother and she agreed to meet us on the mainland in Kyongju, an ancient holy city. The night before she was supposed to come by boat from the island, there was a storm and we were so anxious that she would not be able to make the journey. While we were traveling through Kyongju on our tour bus, our guide received a call from our hotel that Lilly's birth mother, birth father, aunt, and uncle were all waiting for us at the hotel. We immediately left the bus and took a taxi back.

As we pulled up to the hotel, I saw a woman who so resembled my daughter, pacing back and forth in the lobby of the hotel. I saw Lilly's eyes and her mouth; I knew it was her birth mother. I became overwhelmed with emotion. We met her at the entrance and she and I began to cry. Lilly was eleven years old and visibly stunned, completely overwhelmed by the situation. We went into the empty dining room together and there sitting at a table was her birth father, uncle, and aunt. We all sat together, two worlds touching for the first time. Lilly sat next to her birth mother and I sat across from them with Bill and David next to me. At the other end sat her father, quiet and stoic, and her gentle uncle and aunt. Lilly looked like a perfect combination of all of them. Noh-Bu Dol kept staring at Lilly and finally said, "She has my ears and my toes!" Our translator, Judy, was so helpful and kept both families aware of what was being said.

Toward the end of the meeting, Lilly's birth father

asked just one question: "When did you begin the search for us?" Then the uncle instructed Lilly's birth father to hand her an envelope. Inside was two hundred dollars. In the Korean culture, it was a matter of honor that he should give Lilly this money. Then we took a group picture of Lilly and her birth family. Her father said good-bye and her uncle ran to catch the boat back to the island. Her aunt and mother arranged to stay the night into the next day. We took a walk to go to dinner together and the aunt kept calling out to strangers in an excited voice. I asked our translator what she was saying. "She is telling all these strangers that this is a great day because she has been reunited with her family member." When we returned from dinner, all the other adopted children rushed over to Lilly with great excitement. It seemed they all had one question for her: "Why did she give you up for adoption?"

The next day we toured the old city and as Noh-Bu Dol was ready to leave, she put her arm around Lilly and asked me to take a picture. Lilly looked uncomfortable and remained stiff as her birth mother embraced her. One day after we'd returned to New York, Lilly and I were walking down the street. We were holding hands and she looked up at me and said, "You know, I don't really look like her. I look like you."

We unsuccessfully tried to find David's birth parents for the next several years. Just when we thought it would not be possible, a miracle happened. A few years after our first visit to Korea, we received a phone call from

Mrs. Kim at the adoption agency. She asked whether she could bring some social workers from Korea to our home because they wanted to meet a family that had adopted from Korea. We said of course, and they arrived promptly at six o'clock. The three lovely ladies sat on our living room couch; they spoke very little English but were obviously gentle and kind. They asked to see David's adoption file and I put it down in front of one of the ladies. I served them coffee and then I went to get a match to light the candle on the table in front of them. As I approached with the matches, Mrs. Park began yelling, "There is light." I looked at her and said, "Yes, I'm going to light the candles."

"No!" she shouted, "There is hope, this woman took David out of his mother's arms when she relinquished him to the adoption agency." I stood frozen; I couldn't believe this miracle. Of all the people in the world to be sitting on our couch, here was the one person who could help me find his birth parents. We knew at that moment that we had to return to Korea.

On our second visit to Korea, we visited Ulleungdo, the island to which Lilly's birth family had escaped in 1900 when the Japanese and the Chinese had invaded Korea. Because they were scholars, their lives were endangered. I began to sing "Bali Hai" from the musical South Pacific as the boat approached the island because it looked so tropical and beautiful. Lilly was a bit mortified at my rendition. When we disembarked, several Korean women began to bow down to me. Lilly's birth mother met us at the boat and took us to her home above the gas station. For the next five days, we visited Lilly's relatives all over this volcanic island. Every single time we called upon a new home, Noh-Bu Dol insisted that we bring a watermelon with us.

While climbing up and down the mountains, we could see the squid drying on racks from afar, all over the island. We passed women picking roots from within volcanic rock to sell at the marketplace and we climbed rope ladders along the mountainside. We stopped at a large rock outcropping called Western Rock because it looked like a man with a large nose. Bill got out and pro-filed his own nose next to the rock. We all laughed about it and got back in the car, with our watermelon, to visit the next relative.

We traveled by boat and fed shrimp chips to seagulls that swooped down and retrieved the chips from our hands. We reached a tiny island called Bamboo Island, where there were only three inhabitants. We met two of them. I felt like le petit prince, who travels to different planets and finds unusual happenings. Most Korean people have never visited this island and when we left, we knew we were lucky to experience this unique place and to give Lilly the opportunity to see her origins. I also felt a tug of guilt for taking Lilly back to her place of origin for the second time in her life. Her birth mother was so foreign to me, but the sadness in her eyes was so human that I felt moved and sad for her loss and my gain. David was fidgety and seemed adrift. Lilly's body seemed to freeze again when her birth mother gave her a good-bye embrace. There were so many muddy feelings under the smiles and kisses.

We had been told by the social worker that David's birth mother could not see him because her husband would throw her out if he knew about David. I felt that he would never have the opportunity that Lilly had to complete the circle of his life. I tried to explain all the cultural restrictions that were on his birth mother but I always felt frustrated and incomplete in my explanations. How could I possibly make him feel better about this terrible situation, there was no greater rejection. But when we were in Ulleungdo, having lunch on top of a mountain, our translator, Judy, received a miraculous phone call. "Sara, it's for you," she said, and immediately handed over her cell phone.

"Ms. Lavner?" asked the voice on the other end. "I'm the new social worker assigned to your family. I'm calling from Seoul and I have just learned that David's birth mother has changed her mind."

"She has?" I smiled at Bill. "We will head to Seoul immediately."

When we returned to Seoul, we learned that David's birth mother had been misinformed about the day we were to meet. We decided to continue our tour and head to Japan and would meet up with her on our way back through Korea en route to New York.

At the end of our trip, when we reached the airport in Tokyo, we were told that because of immigration regulations and lack of time, we would not be able to get to the main terminal to meet David's birth mother. In distress over this new development, my mind shuffled back and forth over what to do. Bill and I decided that we had to make it to the terminal no matter what they said. When we got off the plane in Korea, we begged the immigration officials to let us out into the terminal, if only for a few minutes. A stranger helped us translate our desperate pleas, and after much arguing, the immigration officials let us through.

We looked over the sea of strangers, the clock ticking in my head, and there in the distance stood a small woman who looked like David. As we neared, I saw tears rolling down her cheeks as she glimpsed David walking beside us. We only had twenty minutes with her.

"Be good and listen to your parents," she said as she held him close.

David couldn't react. Time, space, culture, and connection seemed to squeeze together. There was no time to hesitate or pause; we were all on the edge of our seats, soaking up every feeling and impression. She opened her small purse and gave me a white hairpin with tiny crystals and she gave David two Korean dolls, a man and a woman in traditional Korean dress. We knew we would never see her again.

CHAPTER 28

Back home, while working at the hospital, I met a wonderful music therapist named Janet Sullivan who encouraged me to become a psychoanalyst and to begin studying at her institute. I began to study psychoanalysis and meet with patients. After six years I graduated as the first drama therapist in New York City to also be a psychoanalyst. At my graduation, I recited two poems, "The Jabberwocky" from Alice in Wonderland and "Patterns" by Amy Lowell. One represented the maze of our individual minds and the other represented all the patterns in which human beings get stuck. This recitation summed up for me much of the work that I was exploring with my patients and within myself. Once, I heard a scientist on television explain his work with black holes. "How difficult your job is to explore the black holes of space," commented the reporter. "Oh no, it is nothing next to the human mind." It seemed that I had found a fascinating and challenging profession where all of my skills would be used while I was helping others.

After graduating, I met a woman named Bonnie who invited me to share her office suite. The office I was to take over was painted a tacky bubble-gum pink, but I was able to envision a transformation. I loved the big windows, streams of direct sunlight, and the interesting shadows of the space. It had a working fireplace and was twice as large as most therapists' offices. I had just bought three colorful flowerpots for plants and used them as my jumping-off point in decorating the whole room. I painted it cream and white and put art on the walls and displayed the kimono that Bill's father had given me on the first night that I met him. Bill was afraid that I didn't have enough patients to afford the rent and I thought, Build it and they will come. I went down to the lobby and saw an ad posted by someone who wanted to rent an office two days a week. I called her and instantly I had a tenant and I was able to afford the rent. Whenever my patient load decreased, I would just close my eyes and will new patients to come and work with me. Invariably, they would arrive.

In this new profession, I still felt unsteady in my confidence. I turned to my mentor at NYU, Professor Robert Landy, who became a great supporter. At times, the admiration and acknowledgment of my skills as a therapist seemed falsely given, a perception that stemmed from how I was treated in my family. I still have those moments of doubt, but I pause, breathe, and say thank you.

By this time, Lilly was in high school and doing well

and David was in junior high, doing highly creative things but struggling. Bill was experiencing success as a publisher and decided to go from trade publications to commercial, ultimately landing a job at a famous magazine. Bill began to experience terrible stress and I found myself worrying about his health. We had planned a vacation with the children to Tuscany before he took his new job, but when we were about to leave, they tried to pressure him not to go. I insisted that he needed a break from all the politics and frustration that assaulted him daily at work, so off we went to the beautiful Italian countryside. We lived in a stone house in a small village with tall cypress trees visible from our shuttered windows. There were vineyards nearby and we ate lots of pasta and became friends with a little black cat we called Midi. When we returned to New York, Bill was soon laid off from his new job. He was devastated. I felt angry at how he was treated. At the time, Lilly was in her senior year of high school looking at colleges and David was in his freshman year at the High School of Art and Design. We immediately went from the steady to the unsteady.

Then September 11 befell our city. I was in my office with twelve women at a business meeting when we heard a very loud sound. From the corner of my office, one of the women saw papers flying in the distance and then started screaming. We all turned to see the fires of the first plane. We turned on the radio and heard it was an accident. For some reason, I knew it wasn't. One of the women was a minister and she brought us all into a prayer circle. Suddenly, we heard screams from the rooftops all over Greenwich Village and we saw the second fire. The women started screaming; some knew people who worked at the World Trade Center and one lived nearby in Battery Park City. They all began to leave my office and when I was the only one left, I turned to look out the window where my plants sat on the ledge, green and eager. The first building came down like a sandcastle. I called Bill at home and ran to meet him. We embraced and then got in the car to pick up our son at his school; our daughter was able to take the train home. The streets were filled with people walking uptown and by the next day no cars were allowed below Fourteenth Street. The wind was blowing toward Brooklyn, so it took three days before the smell arrived in the Village. It was a dark, damp, and poisonous smell that made you want to gag. On the second night, everyone took a candle and came into Washington Square Park. We all sat quietly in the darkened park as the many flames flickered in the late summer air.

In October, Bill began to have some balance issues. He went to a neurologist and as we waited weeks for the results, his brother Michael died. As we were getting ready to leave for Michael's memorial service, Bill's neurologist called. I handed the phone to Bill and in an instant I saw his expression completely change. Then he quietly moved to the bedroom and closed the door. When he emerged a few minutes later, he came over to me. "The doctor says that I have a mass on my spine and that I must go immediately to the hospital." It seemed as though I actually ceased breathing, both of us standing frozen in the hallway, a seizing silence around us. "I have to go to my brother's memorial service," he said. "I just don't think we should tell anyone."

"Of course," I quickly agreed, and that was all I said. I wanted to say so many things in that moment. I wanted to confess the acute panic that was taking over my body and my intense fear and my desire to repress it all. We went downstairs where the children were waiting for us and jumped into a taxi. I stared out the window, trying to breathe again.

When we arrived at the service, I went over to the bar and poured myself half a glass of vodka and drank it straight. The service began and Bill spoke of his brother, who was a brilliant, handsome, and complicated man. He had been a heroin addict for seventeen years and then recovered, found out he had contracted HIV, and later was diagnosed with hepatitis C. When Bill finished his speech, we tried to gather our things so we could leave for the hospital. We asked Monte, Bill's other brother, and Ellen, Michael's wife, to come into one of the private rooms with us.

"The doctor called me," Bill said in a surprisingly steady voice, "and told me that I have a mass on my spine. So, Sara and I have to leave for the hospital." Bill looked down as if receiving the news himself for the first time and not knowing the next thing to say. "I'm sorry," he said, looking up.

The next day Bill was admitted to the hospital. The

doctors operated for four hours straight and finally, when the head doctor approached us in the waiting room, he said it would take two more hours to see whether Bill was paralyzed. I went home and cleaned the house. I decided to vacuum the carpet in the living room, sucking up all the gray cat hair. I put the dishes in the dishwasher, turned the dial, and started the cycle. I kept thinking that if I could just get the house in order, then everything would follow suit. I could control the mess.

When I returned to the hospital, I visited Bill in the ICU, kissed him gently on his cheek, and said, "I'll be right back." I desperately needed to know whether Bill had moved his toes. I ran to the nurse. "Yes, he did," she reported briskly.

Then I went back to Bill's bedside and embraced him. I thought, I can do this. I can get through this. He can move his toes. Everything is going to be fine. Our family will be okay. He can move his toes.

It took another week for the doctors to analyze the tumor removed from his spine. Bill was still recovering in the hospital and I was there visiting him when the doctor and his nurse came into the room to tell us the results. "It is cancerous. It is a chondrosarcoma. It is rare that it would be on the spine," he continued, "and the only treatment is an operation in which we would remove the vertebrae and make new vertebrae with pelvic bone. I have never done this operation but I can assist my colleague who has done it before." He and the nurse left the room and Bill and I looked at each other. He began to cry but quietly gathered himself. "I can't believe this has happened," he whispered, labored. I wanted to fall down and bang the floor, but instead I held him and said, "We'll find the best doctor in the world to do this and you will be okay. You will be okay."

We decided to go to the best cancer hospital in the world. We met with one of the few surgeons who could perform this operation. He was incredibly confident and reassured us that all would be fine. He was tall, with an aquiline nose, neatly coiffed white hair, piercing blue eyes, and a soft Irish accent. He was quite accomplished. We were hopeful.

The morning of the operation, Bill woke me at three o'clock.

"Sara," he whispered, "it's pouring outside."

I looked out the window, but the sky was clear. Then I noticed that the wall facing our bed was all wet. There was a sound of gushing water coming from the floor above us. A thick gray line appeared on the wall, from ceiling to floor. There was a hard knock on the door. The firemen soon charged in, looking immense and strong, the last frontier heroes. They looked in our bedroom, noticed that the source was above us, and left to go upstairs to stop the gush of water. I sat quietly in the kitchen.

"Oh, this is a good sign," Bill said from the bed. "It went to another apartment, not ours." I said nothing. Was our life going to be flooded with terrible tragedy?

Would our family break like the pipe in the wall? I pushed these thoughts out of my mind and hurried to prepare for our trip to the hospital.

At five in the morning we left for the hospital. We were shepherded into a waiting room of about thirty people. Then we all traveled up to the operating floors in a very large gray steel elevator. It seemed we were all heading straight to some other celestial realm; even though we didn't know one another, we were all on the same voyage.

Shortly after we arrived at Bill's bed, he was helped into his hospital gown. I climbed up onto his very high bed and sat with him as we waited for the doctor. The sheets were stiff with starch under me. Then a nurse entered and told me to go to the waiting room. We kissed good-bye. I told Bill, "I'll be here waiting for you when you wake up. I love you."

For the next seven hours I sat with Bill's brother, my sister-in-law, and our friends Marci, Robert, Tamar, and Dick. As the sun filled the room, more people came in. The sunlight streamed in and rested on the tension painted on all our faces; we were connected but without words. We would catch glimpses of one another, wondering about one another's stories. When someone was called, everyone quickly turned around, hoping to hear good news. As the sun went down, the room slowly emptied out and became grayer. No one called my name for seven hours. We took over a section near the edge of the windows. Three hours turned to five, and at the seventh hour, when our patience was wearing thin, the two main doctors came into the now darkened room and asked me to follow them. They took me and Monte into a small room nearby. One doctor stood against the wall with his head down, the other told me to sit down across from him.

"Your husband is paralyzed," he said softly but clearly.

I could feel myself falling forward, my pocketbook slipping from my lap. Quickly, the doctor grabbed me by the shoulders and shook me gently. I revived, my head feeling incredibly heavy.

"Please," he asked, "give me permission to do another operation to correct it."

"Do it right away," I answered instantly, my balance restoring.

"I want you to come see him before he is operated on."

Monte and I shuffled back to our family and friends in the waiting room. We told them that we had to go up to see Bill before his next operation. We told them he was paralyzed. Then Monte and I silently walked to the large bank of elevators. When we got into the elevator, I turned to him. "I have to be strong right now for Bill." A woman in the elevator, holding balloons, turned to me and said, "Yes, you do. My seven-year-old daughter just died." I stared into her soft eyes. She seemed so matter-of-fact, it was hard to believe her composure. Then the elevator doors opened and I stumbled out.

I stood for a moment in a wide corridor with Monte holding my hand. We were just outside the operating room. Suddenly, Bill was wheeled out to be with us. His face was swollen and he looked unconscious. I touched his hand, bent down, and whispered in his ear that I loved him. I wanted him to look at me but his eyes stayed closed. Then they wheeled him away into the operating room. I turned sharply and began to punch the air with my fists; I wanted to hit something or someone. Then the doctor appeared and I let my arms fall to my side. He disappeared into the operating room.

Another four hours went by and everyone was gone except Monte and Ellen. Tamar and Dick went to my house to make dinner for Lilly and David. Finally, the doctor came down in his white coat; he looked weary and devastated. "It was too late, I'm sorry. He is now quad-riplegic." Slowly, I rose from my seat and walked out of the hospital with the doctor. I noticed he was wearing a tailored navy-blue cashmere coat. He saw me to a cab. It was midnight.

When I got home, David and Lilly were asleep. I warmed some milk and spooned in some cognac. I lay down in our bed as Henry, my white and gray cat who always slept at my feet, now came and curled up next to my side. We fell asleep, close together.

When I got up the next day to make breakfast for the children, I decided not to tell them that their father was paralyzed. Lilly had exams. I told them that their father was fine.

I rushed to the hospital. Bill was in the ICU, unconscious, with tubes coming out many parts of his body. He did not respond to my words of comfort and he seemed more like a machine than my husband. Pieces of him had been taken away and replaced by the mechanical parts that were sustaining his life. Friends came by and when I gave them permission to see him, they came out of the ICU and fell into each other's arms. Bill's heart was skipping beats and his sugar levels were going haywire. I became so aware of his body, how we are such complex electrical and chemical beings. After about three days, Bill regained consciousness and the doctor asked me to tell him that he was paralyzed.

I went into Bill's room, and in a raspy voice, he asked me how the operation had gone. I took a breath.

"Bill, you are paralyzed."

"What can I move?"

"Right now you are quadriplegic and you can't move your hands or legs, but that may change in the next few months. There could be more movement." There was a deep silence in his eyes, as if he did not hear me. Finally, he whispered, "I'm paralyzed," and I leaned over to kiss him.

CHAPTER 29

That night, I awoke in a startled state, almost thrown upward. I had dreamed that I was wearing the helmet of a general. The dark green dome seemed to swallow my head, but somehow it still fit me. I was the only one who could save my family now. I had to stand up and walk and they had to follow me.

I had to devise a whole new strategy: find a new home in a building with an elevator, figure out how to pay the bills and where I would find the money, decide whether to sue the hospital, find a lawyer, keep my job, and, somehow in the midst of this upheaval, comfort my children.

After the opperation, we lost the friendship of two couples whom we had known for many years. They were so disturbed by how extreme our situation had become and did not have the inner strength to stand with us and face this new reality. For someone to become paralyzed in one moment seemed like a threat. If it could happen to Bill, it could happen to anyone. Becoming paralyzed is so definitive, it completely alters lives, and everything in life seems to become black and white. We saw the reactions from our friends range from very hurtful to loving. We were surrounded by love and lack of love.

On the third day, I asked Lilly to meet me at my office. I knew that I had to tell her seperately from David because he was beginning to be more disconnected from all of us. She met me and on our way to dinner, I told her. She doubled over, crying. I asked her whether she wanted to see her father, but I didn't want to push her because he was so ill. I didn't know whether she could handle seeing her strong and resilient father in this new position. But she gathered up her courage and went with her boyfriend, Adam, and sang to Bill while Adam played the guitar. David had changed, he seemed more fragile and said that he didn't want to go to the hospital. He was becoming more isolated and contrary, so I accepted that he wasn't able to deal with coming to the hospital.

After three months, we had moved to an apartment near Ground Zero. Many buildings were scarred and many stayed closed for months. About half of the people who had lived in the apartment complex we moved to had escaped New York, never to return. The rents in the area went down by 40 percent and I took the first apartment that I saw. We began to see this area rebuild as we, too, began to rebuild our lives.

A month later, after four months in rehabilitation, Bill came home. Bill had learned to steer his wheelchair with his breath. At first, he was afraid to go outside. One day, after about two weeks, he suddenly turned to me. "I want to buy a new TV." His intense resolve surprised me. "Let's go to J&R," he declared. But his health aide would not have it. "You cannot go more than two blocks from your home, this is not possible!"

Although I knew he was nervous about venturing outside, I also knew that this was a pivotal moment in his recovery. He needed to accept his new life. The store was many blocks away and some of the streets' curbs had no indentations for a wheelchair. Bill went into the road and almost went crashing into a crowd of people. I just took a deep breath and kept saying to myself, Oh my God, he will do it. Finally, we got to the store, bought the TV, and went back home.

Over the next months, Bill began to venture outside more while gaining the confidence he needed to live a mobile life as a quadriplegic man. Our family also began to adjust and learn to live together again. We were becoming a new family and at the same time, we were just as we always were.

Bill began to reach out to the world and became a mentor to people who were newly paralyzed. We purchased a special van, with the financial help of friends, that enabled me to drive Bill all over the city. One day, he told me that he wanted to go skydiving with people from his support group who also were paralyzed. At first I thought about the risks involved, but when I saw how important this outing was to him, I could not let my feelings get in the way of his desires.

* * *

As I looked up in the sky for Bill to come out of the clouds, I thought of how I had emerged in my own life, from my weary Brooklyn days, to the opulent and complicated world of Claude Picasso, to leaving it all to create the family I had always wanted. Then I could see dark shapes, like soaring birds, fill the sky. I watched these brave paralyzed men who were strapped to burly instructors float down to the earth in multicolored parachutes, broad as rainbows. I knew all I had gone through now led me to this exact spot, watching my husband taking flight. There was nowhere else I would rather be.

EPILOGUE

A friend called to tell me that Claude's mother, Françoise Gilot was having a gallery show in Manhattan. I knew I had to attend the opening. I called two girl-friends and asked them to go with me. I felt that I needed some support; after all, the last time I had seen Françoise Gilot was in a courtroom thirty years ago when she had testified against me. I called the gallery to ask whether Françoise would be at the opening.

"Yes, Ms. Gilot will be here," said the voice on the phone.

"And will you be expecting her son, Claude?" A moment.

"No, I don't think so." I hung up the phone. I was not going to run into Claude. I was relieved.

My friends and I walked up the two flights of stairs in what felt like a dilapidated building on skid row. A narrow gray stairway led up to an expansive loft painted brilliant white and bedecked with the colorful paintings of Françoise Gilot. I looked around the crowded room, but didn't see Françoise. Then, over in the far corner, I glanced at a very old woman in a red and black suit with heavy black shoes. I moved toward her and recognized the piercing green eyes, bright as emeralds. I knew it was Françoise. I took a deep breath and went over to her. She looked so old, not the black-leather-pants-and-slim-black-turtleneck-wearing woman I had met forty-two years earlier at the airport.

"Hello, it's Sara," I said as I looked down into her eyes. She seemed confused and again I said, "It's Sara, Claude's wife, Sara." Then her brow lifted a bit and her eyes softened; she focused in with greater intensity. As a smile began to take shape she said, "Oh, Claude just walked in." I turned around and saw the back of Claude in a slim charcoal suit. I excused myself and crossed the gallery floor. This was an unthinkable moment; I thought that I would never see him again. Over the years, I had tried to contact him because I needed some closure, and I failed every time, but now he was a few feet away and all I had to do was go over to him. I felt my body freeze—first my hands were cold and then my chest was stiff—but I had to find a way to keep moving toward him. He could say something hateful. He could just dismiss me. I breathed in deeply.

Claude was talking to two very tall people, a man and a woman. They seemed to be having a serious discussion, so I stood close by their side. Finally, I decided to gently interrupt their conversation.

"Hello," I said. "It's Sara." Claude turned to me. His eyes went in and out of focus for a quick moment. Suddenly, he grabbed me and hugged me very tightly, the thirty years disappearing in an instant. We could not take our eyes off each other. He said quickly, "I didn't know how to find you!" His face brightened as if a lamp had been lit from behind his eyes. "My doorman just told me he knows someone who knows you."

"I'm married and have two children that we adopted from Korea."

"Yes, I know." He nodded.

"I'm a drama therapist and psychoanalyst." He smiled and leaned in closer.

"That's a good job for you."

My body relaxed. I was reconnecting with an old, dear friend who knew me well. Then he said, "People told me about the children."

"Who told you?"

"Tony Rosenthal or Richard Kazak," he answered, "I'm not sure. They didn't know how to find you!" I couldn't believe he was trying to find me for all those years. I had a fantasy that in all the years we were apart he tried to get my attention by naming the Citroen Xsara Picasso car after me.

My two friends stood nearby and Claude's young Swiss girlfriend stood next to him, not knowing who I was and what was happening. Claude and I just kept inhaling each other, not looking away for one second.

He had some wrinkles under his eyes but overall he looked healthy, handsome, and happy. Finally, he turned to his girlfriend and told her in French that I was his first wife. She looked at me, and giggled, saying, "You are blushing." I started to feel uncomfortable

"I need a drink," I said.

"Yes, we all need a drink," Claude stated, and I went alone to the bar.

I was already light-headed from the waves of adrenaline coursing through my body. I gulped the wine, needing something to soothe my jitters, to calm my jumping heart. The colorful canvases lining the walls seemed to swirl in a psychedelic trip. I felt dizzy and I needed to walk around.

Gazing into the bright abstract shapes, I was quite impressed that Françoise, at ninety years old, could still produce art. I looked over at Claude, who looked half-buried in the throng of people surrounding him. I feel out of place -- what was I doing here?-- I knew that this meeting was fragile.

I circled the room, wandered among the rich greens, browns, and blues of the paintings and thought about how different Françoise's work had become. I noticed her work was now less derivative of Picasso's and more her own. And in this moment, thirty years later, standing in a room of art with my ex-husband and his mother, I realized that I had come into my own. I was not Mrs. Picasso anymore. I was the creator of my own life. I was a professional, a wife, a mother, and a caretaker.

I knew it was time to go, to go back to where I had come from. I was elated to receive Claude's embrace but I was eager to leave. I needed to go home.

I went over to Françoise to tell her how much I liked her work.

"I'm sorry that I didn't recognize you," she whispered in her unsteady voice.

"I understand," I assured her, "it's been a long time. I just want you to know that I'm sorry for any pain that I may have caused you or your family in the past. It is so nice to see you again and your beautiful art." Françoise nodded and I left her.

I walked over to Claude. He whispered in my ear, "I will see you next week." I gave him my card and felt my cheeks warm under the gallery lights.

"Good." And I left.

I wanted more. I wanted to know everything. I wanted to sit and talk to him and tell him everything that had happened to me in the last thirty years and to hear what had happened to him. His shining face and our embrace kept flashing back to me. Would he actually call? Why hadn't he received the two letters that were delivered to him? Did he really want to find me? He appeared earnest and sincere. Was I just imagining it all? I didn't understand the rush of feelings that I was experiencing. Then I felt fear dipping into me, the thought that I would never see him again. It all seemed like a dream—a good dream in a time machine.

The next day I kept seeing his face in front of me: smiling, laughing, full of energy, and happy to see me. I had no control over what would happen next, it was up to him whether we would ever see each other again. It was as if the memory were a cloud formation, created for a few moments, only to break apart and lose shape. How special it would be to finally talk and begin to understand what had happened between us. But he was not someone who was necessarily interested in looking back. Would he feel like he couldn't trust me? Would his anger toward me return? Would he laugh to hear that I lived around the corner from Picasso Pizza? Or would he cut me off again? I prepared myself for this possibility.

Bill said, "If he doesn't call after he said that he would, then that will show something important about his character." Yes, I had to agree.

Four days after seeing Claude, I had a dream. I was trying to go somewhere and I had many different bags with me. Suddenly I remembered that I had forgotten my little red bag with my ID and money. I awoke feeling disturbed. The little red bag was my heart and during the turmoil of the last four days, I had forgotten to check my heart, to make sure it was safe. I had lost it to Claude, to my past, and now I knew that I had to find it again.

Every time the phone rang or I opened my e-mail, I wanted to hear his voice or read his words. As the days passed, my hope kept diminishing until finally it was the end of the week. He never called.

In the days since, in the quiet of my Connecticut summer retreat, I no longer feel the acute hurt but understand that my meeting with Claude was like a painting: a moment in time captured on a canvas that stands alone. I turn to the new painting of my life, a still life colored with rich love. I see the brushstrokes of friendship and the imprint of a brave husband, a sensitive daughter, and an artistic son coping with his illness. I am loved and I love, I know who I am and I know what I need. The days end but the sky glows like a bright azure acrylic. I sip my tea as the vanishing sun glitters on the river.

ACKNOWLEDGEMENTS

I want to gratefully acknowledge the never-ending encouragement from my daughter, Lilly Lavner. For my son, David Lavner and my husband, Bill, I want to thank them for teaching me more about love and patience than I had ever experienced. I want to thank my friend Robert Landy, my mentor at New York University, who never stopped asking me, "When will you start writing the book?" For her love and ability to share her wisdom with me, I want to thank my dear friend Marci Sutin Levin. I am grateful to my family and friends for their enthusiasm and support, which helped me to tell my story. I want to express my deep gratitude to the poet Thomas Dooley, my friend and editor, who taught me about writing, poetry, and many more things during our Friday morning breakfasts.

ABOUT THE AUTHOR

Sara Lavner was born in Brooklyn and lives in Manhattan. She worked as a professional actress and maintains a private practice as a drama therapist and psychoanalyst. This is her first book.

Made in the USA
Las Vegas, NV
22 April 2022

47866494R00125